Mrs G Cole
14 Wode Close
Waterlooville
PO8 0HX

CW00542725

Assault on Germany

Assault on Germany

The Battle for Geilenkirchen

Ken Ford

Pen & Sword
MILITARY

First published in Great Britain in 2009 by
Pen & Sword Military
an imprint of
Pen & Sword Books Ltd
47 Church Street
Barnsley
South Yorkshire
S70 2AS

ISBN 978-1-84884-098-0

The right of Ken Ford to be identified as Author of this Work has been asserted by them in accordance with the Copyright, Designs and Patents Act 1988.

A CIP catalogue record for this book is available from the British Library.

Typeset in 11pt Ehrhardt by
Mac Style, Beverley, E. Yorkshire

Printed and bound in the UK by MPG Books Group

Pen & Sword Books Ltd incorporates the imprints of Pen & Sword Aviation, Pen & Sword Maritime, Pen & Sword Military, Wharncliffe Local History, Pen and Sword Select, Pen and Sword Military Classics and Leo Cooper.

For a complete list of Pen & Sword titles please contact
PEN & SWORD BOOKS LIMITED
47 Church Street, Barnsley, South Yorkshire, S70 2AS, England
E-mail: enquiries@pen-and-sword.co.uk
Website: www.pen-and-sword.co.uk

Dedication

William Charles Ford

1907–1968

Peter Arthur Lanning

1923–1985

Contents

Author's Acknowledgements

I would like to extend my sincere thanks to all who have helped me in the preparation of this book.

First, I wish to acknowledge the invaluable help of all the real life heroes who participated in the battle. I give special thanks to the following who were able to give information about Operation Clipper:

British 43rd Infantry Division
Ron Barber, Sam Beard, Major-General H.A. Borradaile, Douglas Burdon, William Caines, Colonel Michael Concannon, Louis Dawes, John Denison, George Drake, W.S. Drew, Maurice Edwards, Algy Grubb, Arthur Hitchcock, Brigadier Michael Lonsdale, Major George Loosley, J.L. Meredith, F.J. Petrie, Colonel John Ricketts, Colonel D.I.M. Robbins, Major Len Roberts, Cliff Roberts, Dan Robertson, Dick Rutter, Pat Spencer Moore, Brigadier George Taylor, Eric Tipping, Pat Tucker, Tony Walsh, Lieutenant-Colonel R.S. Williams Thomas, Sir David Willcocks

Sherwood Rangers Yeomanry
Major Peter Selerie, Rev Leslie F. Skinner

US 84th Infantry Division
Wendell E. Albert, Louis Alicandri, Lee C. Allen, Zeke Almaguer, Harry Amoroso, Major Kenneth Ayer, Everett Blackert, Clyde Boden, Gil Bradham, Christian A. Braun, James D. Callahan, Royce Clements, Joseph Curtis, Charles W. Dunn, R.L. Ellarson, C.B. Ellison, Ed Epstein, Captain George Felton, Frank Freese, Irving Friedlander, Joe Garcia, George W. Green, Jack Gromer, Floyd Hargus, Richard Howland, Howard H. Hyle, J. Horkin, John Housend, Paul Howeter, Edward W. Keen, Dempsey Keller, Colonel Fritz Kramer, Bill Knutson, James Kurtzweil, Thomas R. Kyle, David C. Laing, Mack Lawson, Colonel Harold P. Leinbaugh, Ray Lindsey, Roy Long, Clarence E. Love, James E. Meehan, Dan McCullen, William Miller Jr, John J. O'Malley Jr, Governor

Arch E. Moore, John F. Mulligan, Frank Pinto, Don Poorman, Robert Rachlin, John T. Reed, William P. Reed, Richard J. Roush, Walter E. Ruff, Frank Ruzica, August E. Schmidt Jr, David Skoler, William Sofield, Gene Solfelt, Jack Sutherland, Rev Dr Harold Weaver, Howard Weckel, Colonel William Wootton Jr, Maurice Wolfson, Frank Zeno

US 102nd Infantry Division
John Barnett, Raymond Bertie, Edward Brim, Robert Brockman, Gordon Caesar, Morton Chalef, Irvin M. Citron, Doug Connaher, Edwin S. Dojka, Daniel S. Ebling, John D. Emerich, Robert Enkelmann, George Fogle, Benjamin Gerber, Aubrey Green, Pasqual Guarez, John C Harber, Jim Harris, Erivin F. Hoffman, John E. Johnstone, John J. Kennedy, Wallace J. Katz, Leland F. King, Frank Kuplin, Francis Mead, John H. Middlebrooks, Richard S. Morse, Paul Proshuto, Brigadier-General Wilson R. Reed, Albert E. Schwabacher, Charles Schell, Arnold Short, Edward L. Souder, Chet Twentyman, Jack Vorhies, Benny Wiseman

US 28th Infantry Division
Frank Krackow

US 104th Infantry Division
Ken Parsons

US 2nd Armored Division
Charles Hinds

US 629th Tank Destroyer Battalion
Russell Brown

US 6th Tactical Air Support Squadron
T.M. Bliss

I wish also to thank the Imperial War Museum, London; the Public Records Office, London; the National Archives, Washington; the US Army Military History Institute, Carlisle Barracks; the *American Legion* magazine; the *Veterans of Foreign Wars* magazine; the Railsplitters Society and the 102nd Infantry Division Association for their assistance during my research.

I would also like to acknowledge all the kind assistance and hospitality I received during my visit to Germany: Leo and Annie Schreinemacher, Willi and Anna Offermann, Hans Kramp, Peter Brauweiler, Agnes Schummertz, Peter Porscheu, and Josef and Henny Buchkremer.

I owe a debt of gratitude to all the people who helped me assemble, translate and produce the wealth of details that went into this book: Stephen Schlerath, Sam Muscolino, Franz Kuhoff, Gordon and Cherry Neaves, and especially to John Haswell for the excellent maps.

I am also grateful for permission to use quotations from the following: *The 43rd Wessex Division at War: 1944–1945* by Major General H. Essame; *The First Battalion The Worcestershire Regiment in North West Europe*, by Major D.Y. Watson and *The 84th Infantry Division in the Battle of Germany*, by Theodore Draper.

I would also like, in this new edition, to recognise the local historical research done by my friend Norbert Rosin during the years since the first edition was published. His efforts have given the people of Geilenkirchen, and the NATO servicemen and women stationed nearby, much new information on this important battle. My thanks go to him and his family for the support and hospitality they continue to give during my frequent trips to Germany.

In closing, I offer a very special thanks for the patience and understanding of my wife Valda and my daughters Amanda and Joanne during the preparation of this book.

Ken Ford, 2009

Prologue

It was raining. It had rained every day for the last two weeks. November 1944 was a wet and dreary month. The last leaves of autumn had been blown from the trees and blasted by the violent explosions of shell and fire. The River Wurm meandered aimlessly through a barren north German landscape of small villages, deserted quarries, dense woods and open fields of beet and cabbage. Between the ugly slag heaps, sparse houses and farms lay shattered and broken. The rain had turned the countryside into an ocean of mud. The debris of war lay all around.

Overlooking the desolate scene, a few hundred yards back from the now quiet front line, a fresh faced nineteen year old private stared out from his waterlogged foxhole. He was a long way from his Kentucky home and was new to the battle area, as were the rest of his buddies; the M1 carbine that he clutched tightly across his chest had not yet fired a shot in anger.

The young soldier could hear the sound of a jeep slowly approaching along the narrow muddy lane that led up to his post. He rose out of his trench and took cover behind a tree. The jeep contained three passengers and as it drew near he could see they were not Americans. With his rifle raised ready for action, he ordered the jeep to halt. Pointing his gun at the front seat passenger he demanded, 'Who the hell are you?'

The tall distinguished passenger gingerly stepped out of the vehicle and onto the road. He was dressed in a short overcoat with a woollen scarf tied loosely around his neck. On his head he wore the peaked cap of a British officer displaying the metal cap badge of the Middlesex Regiment. 'I am a Britisher – and what's more, your division has just been placed under my command,' said the passenger.

The American stared incredulously at the Britisher. 'What's your rank?' he demanded. 'A three-star general,' replied the officer. There was a pause as the GI took a deep breath. 'Holy Moses! We don't see many of them up here.'

Lieutenant-General Brian Horrocks was no stranger to the front line. He was an old campaigner of many previous battles throughout three continents and two world wars. Horrocks was visiting his troops at the sharp end to see conditions for himself. But this visit was different; this day he was making history. For the first time in almost two hundred years, a British general was preparing to do battle on German soil.

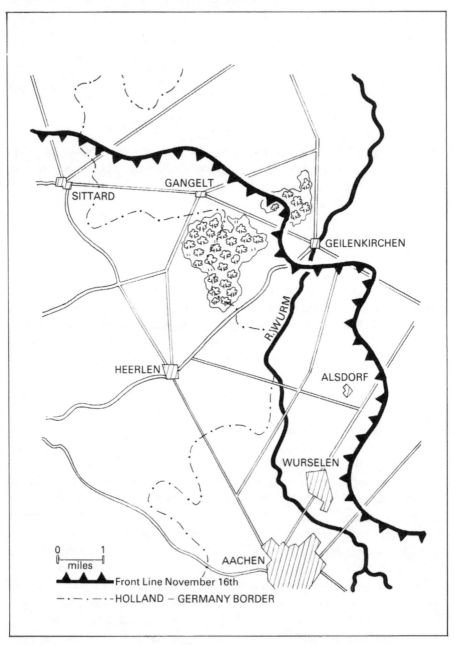

Map 1: The U.S. Ninth Army's Front Line.

Chapter One

The Problem of Geilenkirchen

Throughout the first four years of World War Two, Hitler's 'Westwall', known to the Allies as the Siegfried Line, had achieved a position of awe in the minds of soldiers and politicians. Although much fun had been poked at the static defensive line by the public at large – a popular song proclaimed that it would eventually serve only as a washing line – pre-war Nazi propaganda had done its job most effectively with regard to the military. The Westwall appeared to be an effective barrier to the invasion of Germany.

The 1930s had seen a gradual rise in number of military strategies accepting the relatively new theories concerning the need for mobility in both attack and defence. The principles of fast armoured warfare, supported by aircraft and motorised troops, that had been put forward by men like Fuller and Liddell Hart in England, were quickly taken up by Guderian in Germany and de Gaulle in France. From these early ideas, the blitzkrieg concept of attack was evolved. Hitler eagerly embraced this new ideology and set about building up his armoured formations, together with his own defensive wall that could use mobility and air power to best effect. He employed a different approach to that of the French with their Maginot Line.

While the Maginot principle relied on a seemingly impregnable line of immensely strong fortifications, the Siegfried Line depended upon a system of mutually supporting areas of smaller works to give defence in depth. Once the Maginot Line had been pierced, it would become valueless; the attacking enemy could rapidly fan out through any penetration into the open country beyond. However, any attack against the German Westwall would find its momentum slowed down by increasingly stronger lines of defence. Behind this fortified line, out of reach of the attacking army, an armoured strike force could be assembled ready to unleash a crushing counter-attack. The basis for Hitler's plan of defence was to use his tanks and aircraft to fight a mobile battle within the fortified area where all the advantages favoured the defenders.

The advance positions of the Siegfried Line amounted to no more than a weakly held system of field fortifications comprising of barbed wire, mines and slit trenches. It was to be just strong enough to hold up the attackers until the alarm was raised. About three miles behind this line was a fortified belt capable of much more serious opposition. First, there was a continuous anti-tank obstacle formed either by natural land features such as rivers or lakes, or by lines of 'dragon's teeth' made from concrete and steel. Next, came a zone of barbed wire entanglements and minefields and, finally, clusters of pillboxes and casemates giving each other mutual support through interlocking machine gun and anti-tank gun fire.

Behind the first fortified belt, stretching to a depth of between four and six miles, was an intermediate area of isolated works located at certain critical points. Often, behind this intermediate area, there was another fortified belt of pillboxes and casemates, depending on the lie of the land and the likelihood of attack through it.

However, the reality of the Siegfried Line as it was built in 1938 was somewhat different from the intentions of its designers a few years earlier. It never did reach the strength that had been envisaged during the planning stages. By necessity, it was hurriedly built, often with inferior materials. Nonetheless, its shortcomings were more than made up for by the Nazi propaganda machine. As soon as it neared completion, Joseph Goebbels went to work on the minds of the German people, together with those of its potential enemies.

At home, the German nation was able to build up its military might safe from attack from the western Allies. Abroad, details of the Siegfried Line convinced Britain and France that a successful attack against Germany would be a formidable and risky operation. Thus, by continually overstating its strength and possible effectiveness, Hitler was able, in 1939, to turn his attention east against Poland, secure in the knowledge that his rear was covered by his great Westwall.

At the beginning of November 1944, American troops had been in the area overlooking Geilenkirchen for over six weeks. Advanced units of the First US Army had reached the villages just short of the town during the middle of September. Their arrival in the area marked the end of the great Allied 'blitzkrieg' that had begun, two months earlier, four hundred and fifty miles away in Normandy. The ten weeks of ponderous battles of attrition amongst the confines of the close knit Normandy bocage were over. British and American forces had broken two German armies and effected a break out into the heartland of France. Centre stage was given over to a more mobile type of warfare in which the Allied superiority in mechanised forces could be brought into play. The results were spectacular: armoured spearheads fanned out in all directions and sent the German forces reeling into a disorganised retreat towards the Fatherland. Within a few short weeks, most of France, Belgium and Holland were liberated. Apart from a few isolated incidents, German resistance was slight. This lack of opposition created a euphoric mood among the pursuing armies. There was a feeling prevalent in the Allied camp that the war would be over before Christmas. The enemy was showing clear signs of having been beaten. Then things began to change. Once the Allies crossed over the German border, they brushed up against the Siegfried Line.

The Siegfried Line of September 1944 was not, however, the line of 1940. Continually robbed of its permanent equipment and guns to replenish losses elsewhere, the defences of the Westwall were, by that time, in a sorry state. Hitler had made little attempt to strengthen the line, having based his hopes of being able to stop the Allies' progress eastwards on the lines of the great rivers of France and Belgium. Nonetheless, it did still have its awesome reputation working for it.

That same month, the Supreme Commander of the Allied Expeditionary Force, General Dwight D. Eisenhower saw the line as '...a defensive system that only a well-supplied and determined force could hope to breach.' Eisenhower's assessment of the effectiveness of the line was a pessimistic one, founded on enemy propaganda and inadequate intelligence reports.

The Allies paused at the German border to gain strength and organise their severely stretched lines of communications. It was a mistake; the enemy used the respite to gain time to strengthen its Westwall. New troops were raised by lowering the age of conscription and by combing the factories for surplus manpower. The result was that when the Allies attempted to advance again, they found a defence which was much stronger than expected.

One of the traditional invasion routes into Germany from the Low Countries passed through Charlemagne's ancient city of Aachen. For centuries, the Aachen Gap had been the door by which countless armies had marched into Germany. When Hitler came to build that section of Westwall which ran along the nearby border, the lesson that history afforded him was not lost. The section of line around the city was made into one of the strongest stretches of its entire length. Aachen was encircled by a double band of fortifications, five miles apart. Eight miles north of the city, the two lines joined in a single wide belt of concrete defences along the valley of the River Wurm, passing just to the east of the town of Geilenkirchen.

Advanced units of General Hodge's First US Army had reached the line in front of Aachen during the middle of September. It then took a month for the Americans to capture the city, a month of hard, bloody battle. Even when it was finally taken, only the first band of fortifications had been penetrated. Aachen's stubborn resistance enabled the Germans to reinforce the defences to the east of the city, allowing the Westwall to remain intact as a defensive line.

On 22 October, the newly operational Ninth US Army, commanded by General William Simpson, arrived in the area and set up its headquarters in

Maastricht. It was immediately given the task of holding the left flank of the American forces. Simpson was given control of the section of the line from a point just north of Aachen, to the boundary with General Bernard L. Montgomery's 21 British Army Group at Maeseyck in Holland. Ninth Army had become part of General Omar Bradley's 12 US Army Group.

Four days earlier, on 18 October, the Supreme Commander, General Eisenhower, had met with Montgomery and Bradley to agree the next phase of the war. Eisenhower had decided on a 'broad front' strategy, which meant that all of his forces would advance together, pushing back the Germans all along the front line. In keeping with this decision, he now proposed that both Montgomery and Bradley should attack and capture the Rhineland – that part of Germany between the Dutch border and the River Rhine. Montgomery would attack southeastwards from Nijmegen with his Second British Army, while Bradley attacked eastwards with his First and Ninth US Armies.

Further operations were planned for the remainder of the line: General Patton's Third US Army was to attack towards the Saar, the Seventh US Army towards Karlsruhe and the First French Army towards the Rhine between the Swiss frontier and Mulhouse. This great winter offensive was timed to begin in early November.

No sooner had the advance been planned than problems began to arise. Montgomery was in no position to attack until the approaches to the port of Antwerp had been cleared. The difficult supply situation was such that the opening of the port became the single most important task of the entire campaign at that time. In addition, he was having problems with the enemy near his start line on the Meuse. Consequently, the British attack would be delayed and would not have the strength that was first envisaged.

Bradley was also having trouble. Owing to the length of his two hundred and fifty mile front, and in view of the requirements for Patton's offensive against the Saar, the number of divisions available to him was not as great as he had hoped. A compromise was reached: the British would take over that part of the US line as far south as Geilenkirchen and Montgomery would return to Bradley those American divisions that were serving in the British sectors.

General Simpson had two corps at his disposal for the Ninth Army's part in the attack. First and foremost, was the experienced XIX Corps that had been transferred to him from the First US Army. This corps was to make the main effort with its 2nd Armored, and 29th and 30th Infantry Divisions. Simpson's other corps was the new XIII Corps, which at that time consisted of only the 113th Cavalry Group and the untried 102nd Infantry Division. Further additions were planned, but had not yet arrived: the veteran 7th US Armored Division was still with the British and the 84th Infantry Division was at that moment in transit from its training base in the USA.

On 13 November, XXX British Corps, commanded by Lieutenant-General Brian Horrocks, moved southwards to take over control of seventeen miles of the line previously held by the Ninth US Army. The British now held the northern part of the western front from the North Sea to the outskirts of Geilenkirchen in Germany. The role given to XXX Corps was merely to hold the line in that sector; it had no part to play in the forthcoming offensive.

The path of the River Wurm runs due north from the outskirts of Aachen and then veers north-eastwards at Geilenkirchen. In November 1944, the river marked the boundary of the British and American forces, although the town of Geilenkirchen, sitting astride the Wurm, was assigned to the American sector. The town served as an anchor point on that part of the Siegfried Line, making the surrounding area one of the strongest sections of the whole of Hitler's Westwall. Most of the fortifications were built along the eastern side of the river valley so as to make best use of the high ground.

General Simpson knew that he could not push eastwards and leave Geilenkirchen untaken, for the further he advanced the more insecure his left flank would become. Yet if he included the town in his operation, the momentum of his attack would almost certainly become slowed down by the costly house to house fighting needed to clear the built up area. It would take a lot of effort to complete the job and a lot of manpower, at least one whole division, possibly two. Simpson had only one division available, the inexperienced 84th Division. The whole escapade might well over-extend his front and cause all manner of further problems. Simpson decided that a solution could possibly be found if the British were to agree to a slight shifting of their XXX Corps' boundary.

Lieutenant-General Brian Horrocks was one of the most gifted and respected commanders in the whole of the British Army. He was a veteran campaigner from World War One. He had been a brigade commander in Montgomery's 3rd Division at Dunkirk and went on to command the 9th Armoured Division in England. A short while later, he once again teamed up with Montgomery, this time in North Africa as a corps commander. After being severely injured in Bizerta, he spent a year in hospital recovering from wounds. By July 1944, he was well enough to resume his active service. Montgomery brought him over to France as Commander of XXX Corps in Normandy. He joined it at the time of the 'break out'. Over the next six weeks, XXX Corps became the Second British Army's spearhead in the lightning drive across northern France, Belgium and Holland, that ended at Arnhem. Horrocks now brought his famous XXX Corps next to Simpson in the line at Geilenkirchen.

Horrocks had his headquarters in a town called Beek in Holland, just six miles down the road from Simpson in Maastricht. The Ninth US Army Commander decided to pay a call on his British neighbour and put a proposition to him. Simpson suggested that Horrocks should support the Ninth Army's drive by taking the town of Geilenkirchen for him. Horrocks declined, explaining that as much as he would like to help, he had only one division, the 43rd, at his disposal and that it was clearly a task for which two would be needed. As there was no possibility of persuading Montgomery to loan him any extra troops, he did not see how he could help overcome the problem.

Soon afterwards, Horrocks received an invitation from Simpson to join him at his headquarters for dinner during a visit by the Supreme Commander. Horrocks was already on good terms with Simpson and he knew the Supreme Commander, General Eisenhower, quite well.

The British general was treated to a fine show of hospitality and dined liked a prince. After dinner, in a very relaxed atmosphere, Eisenhower exercised his considerable charm and turning to Horrocks said, 'Well Jorrocks [his nickname], are you going to take Geilenkirchen for us?' Horrocks replied that the spirit was willing, but the flesh was weak. 'I have only the veteran 43rd Division available to me, and that division has taken a terrible pounding since it arrived in Normandy. I couldn't possibly take the town, one of the strongest positions on the Westwall, with just that one division.'

Eisenhower would not take no for an answer. He turned to Simpson, 'Give him one of ours,' he said. 'Sure,' replied the Ninth Army's Commander, and offered the 84th Infantry Division, which was newly arrived from the States. Horrocks protested that the task ahead was going to be difficult. Was it fair, he asked, to send the green division into its first action under the command of a 'limey' general?

The two American generals quickly brushed aside any misgivings that Horrocks had. The English commander soon found himself agreeing to attack Geilenkirchen with the two divisions. The American problem of Geilenkirchen had now become a British one.

Chapter 2

The Wessexmen and the 'Railsplitters'

At 1800 hours on 12 June 1944, in a small Kentish town just a few miles inland from the coastline of the English Channel, a signals officer gave the order to transmit the codeword 'Mary' to all units of a British infantry division. It was a signal that had been long anticipated. The 43rd (Wessex) Infantry Division was ordered to the Channel ports in readiness for its embarkation to France. Its long dreary days of training were over. 'One of the best trained divisions that ever left our shores,' according to Lieutenant-General Brian Horrocks, was off to war.

The British 43rd Division was a Territorial Army infantry division, comprising battalions from most of the county regiments of the West Country of England. In the Dark Ages of English history, these counties made up the Kingdom of Wessex, the Land of the West Saxons: Hampshire, Wiltshire, Dorset, Somerset and Berkshire, and, in later times, Devon and Cornwall. The West Saxons were a warrior people. In the year 825, their king, Egbert, devoted himself to the task of bringing the surrounding kingdoms under his sway. One by one, the realms of the Angles and Saxons fell to him until he commanded the whole of the southern parts of the British Isles. At his death in 839, there was, for the first time, a king and a kingdom of England.

Exactly eleven hundred years later, on 1 September 1939, a distant descendant of King Egbert signed the order for the embodiment of the Territorial Army. In response to this order, broadcast on the BBC by King George VI, men from all over the ancient kingdom of Wessex once again began to assemble for war.

The Wessex Division was not earmarked for immediate mobilisation, so for the first few months of the war the assembled battalions trained with very little proper clothing, equipment or transport. The field regiments of the Royal Artillery had to make do with old, obsolete guns and a motley collection of cars and lorries.

To add to the discomfort, the War Office decided to move all territorial units away from their peacetime areas, to enable training to be conducted without interference from the pleasures and stresses of home life. A great criss-crossing of areas ensued: the Hampshires moved to Dorset, the Dorsets to Wiltshire, the Wiltshires to Somerset, and so on. The Division was then set to begin a period of training which was to last for five years, a time during which it was labelled 'the most over-exercised division in the whole of the British Army.'

In early 1940, better equipment began to arrive in quantity and the Division prepared itself to join the British Expeditionary Force in France. The month of May saw the start of mobilisation, with a move to an area north of London. The expected embarkation, however, did not materialise, for the German Army had made a breakthrough in the Ardennes and could not be held by the British and French Armies. The Allies began to fall back in a great retreat that was to end at Dunkirk.

The remnants of the Expeditionary Force that landed back in England had left all their arms and equipment broken and immobilised on the continent of Europe. The only fully equipped infantry division ready for action in June 1940 was the 43rd (Wessex) Division.

Britain then entered a period, for the first time in more than a century and a half, when the threat of invasion was real. Alone, the country faced the might of the Axis powers now gathering just twenty-five miles away across the English Channel.

The invasion never came. The Battle of Britain took place in the air, not on land. The Royal Air Force was more than a match for the German *Luftwaffe*. Without complete mastery of the skies above England, Hitler did not dare to attempt a seaborne assault with the Royal Navy still at large. The attack was postponed; Hitler turned his attention towards Russia.

The 43rd Division passed the next few years training in Kent and Sussex. Command of the Division was taken over on 2 March 1942 by Major-General G.I. Thomas. With the threat of an invasion receding, Thomas increased the pace of training. A strict disciplinarian, obsessed with perfection, he ran the Division on austere lines, demanding total commitment from all the troops. Taking a lead from Montgomery, Thomas insisted that all ranks should be exposed to the rigours of modern war. The men were to accept privation and physical hardship as part of their normal conditions. Exposure to the elements was to be endured for long periods and their fitness was to be beyond question.

For three long winters, the Division carried out a monotonous series of exercises in Kent. This was a depressing time, in a depressing county, as the divisional historian describes:

More than any other county, owing to its close proximity to France, the constant air raids and its general shabbiness, it reflected the atmosphere of war. It is also undoubtedly the coldest place in the British Isles. The division's main training area was Stone Street, north of Folkestone. All the colder winds from central Europe seem to converge here. It is a tangle of squalid woods and muddy lanes embodying all the nastiest elements of nature at her worst. A midwinter night spent in the open here is calculated to leave no man in doubt as to the reason why the Scandinavian concept of eternal punishment was, unlike the Hebrew, linked with extreme cold and not excessive heat. In real war some shelter from the elements can usually be found. This was not the case with Stone Street. The philosopher who asserted that eternity is beyond human conception never trained with the 43rd Division, otherwise he would have been less dogmatic.

These nine rifle battalions of infantry, together with the regiments of Royal Artillery and Royal Engineers, all originated in the counties of Wessex. As the divisional sign, the 43rd chose the yellow wyvern. This mystical beast, with the head of a dragon, the body of a snake and the feet of an eagle, had been the emblem of the Kings of Wessex since the Dark Ages. It had been borne into battle by the fighting men of the West Country for centuries. Raised by King Harold at Hastings in 1066 against an invasion from Normandy, it was, nine centuries later, destined to be carried back across the channel to Duke William's ancient duchy. Emblazoned on the shoulders of every man, the wyvern was once again used as a battle sign; this time against a different enemy, an enemy who came to regard those who wore it as the 'yellow devils'.

The bulk of the Division were part-time territorials, a grouping together of local men to form an army. Their main allegiance was to their 'mates', and to the Regiment. The British system of county regiments, composed of battalions of men from individual towns or areas, made for a fierce pride in the unit. Each man would never let his mates down. They were all neighbours, they had been to the same schools, danced in the same halls, drank in the same pubs and even dated the same girls. They valued their lives like any other man, but when they were called on to go forward, sometimes against terrible odds, their loyalty to each other made them do so without question.

The US 84th Infantry Division was, in the words of Lieutenant-General Brian Horrocks, 'an impressive product of American training methods which turned out division after division complete, fully equipped and trained for war.' It had to be, for the task facing America when it declared war on Germany and Japan in December 1941 was a monumental one. At that time, the strength of the US Army was 1,686,000 men. By the end of World War Two, it stood at over 8,500,000. The raising of this army from a small, outdated and ill-equipped force into one of the mightiest armies in the world called for a miracle of organisation on an immense scale.

The infantry division during World War Two was the largest self-contained unit capable of acting independently. It comprised all the necessary arms and support to sustain itself in action. The basic American infantry division was very similar to its British counterpart, the main differences being in nomenclature. At its heart were the three rifle regiments (known as brigades in a British division). Each regiment contained three battalions of infantry, each of which contained four companies. These nine battalions were the cutting edge of the division. But for each rifleman in the front line, there was an equivalent member of the division not far behind providing support and services.

The division had its own artillery back-up from three battalions of field artillery. (In the British Army, these battalions were known as field regiments, for example the 94th Field Regiment Royal Artillery was equivalent to a US battalion of field guns.) Other artillery units provided anti-tank and anti-aircraft protection. An American division had a battalion of medium artillery as part of its complement, while the British had such support assigned to it as directed by the Corps.

Divisional engineers supplied the expertise for a wide range of duties and were capable of light bridging operations. Then came the specialists: there were medical, transport, ordnance, electrical and mechanical engineers, education, postal, cash, security and hygiene units, each an important component in the division's goal of self-sufficiency in the line.

The American 84th Division was activated on 15 October 1942. It had, however, a much longer pedigree than this might imply. During World War One, the 84th was referred to as the 'Lincoln' Division, because it was primarily made up of National Guard units from Illinois, Kentucky and Indiana – the Lincoln States. Its original insignia was a red axe on a white background within a red circle, with the name 'Lincoln' above the axe and the number 84 below it. In World War Two, the insignia consisted of a white axe splitting a white rail, on a red circular background. Both insignia recall President Lincoln's use of the axe in his youth. With the addition of a split rail, the division adopted the new nickname of 'Railsplitters'.

On paper the 84th Division was identical to every other American division being shipped out to the front line. A mass-production unit straight off the assembly line. In reality, the division was made up of companies of individuals, and each company had a distinctive outlook. Although there were none of the long regimental traditions that were associated with British units, the average American GI, nonetheless, had a great pride in his outfit. After two years of training together in close company with his buddies, his morale was sky high. The GIs' belief in themselves was as great as any veteran outfit; each believed they were part of 'the best damned rifle company in the goddam' army'.

The make-up of the division was the same as most others, consisting of three infantry regiments: the 333rd, the 334th and the 335th Regiments. Each of these comprised three battalions, numbered 1st, 2nd and 3rd. Initially, it comprised a small cadre of regular NCOs and officers, with the bulk of its complement made up of men drafted into the army – a cross section of adult male America. However, in April 1944, the level of education rose dramatically with the arrival of a contingent of men from the Army Specialised Training Program (ASTP).

The ASTP had been designed to provide a university education for those recruits with an IQ higher than 120 (it only took an IQ of 110 to be eligible for Officers' Candidate School). The idea was to produce a supply of well-educated specialists to fulfil all the US Army's needs during the latter part of what was increasingly becoming a mechanised war.

Unfortunately, the whole programme came to a sudden halt in March 1944 when it was abandoned by the Army. The trainees were shipped off, principally to understrength infantry divisions, to begin new careers as infantrymen. It would be an understatement to say that the ASTP students were not pleased with this development. They were all sufficiently intelligent to have made selection for officers' training school, but had instead found themselves carrying a rifle. In addition, they had to suffer the unwelcome derision of other soldiers as being 'whiz kids'. Richard Howland was one such newcomer and he recalls there being a lot of anger and resentment between the old regulars and the young college kids when he joined the 'Railsplitters'.

After the war, General Herman Beukema, who had been in charge of the programme, called the decision to abandon it a mistake. He agreed the Army had no choice since Congress, in their desire to manage the war, had eliminated the programme appropriations. The result was that the Army was forced to make extremely inefficient use of personnel, but when considering the history and nature of warfare, efficiency and reasonableness seem to be the exception rather than the rule.

Almost two years after the division was first activated, Brigadier-General Alexander R. Bolling took his 84th Infantry Division overseas to war. In September 1944, the 'Railsplitters' set sail for Europe.

Hundreds of new divisions were activated throughout World War Two. Some were successful and ended the war covered in glory, while others had a less fortunate time. Success was measured in battles won or lost. Inevitably, the final judgement came down to how well the commanding general had performed. He took the glory, and the blame, for the performance of his men on the battlefield.

Brigadier-General Alexander R. Bolling was born in Philadelphia, Pennsylvania, on 28 August 1895, the only son of a successful doctor. The young Alexander was determined to make the military his career. After taking a very tough entrance examination, he managed to obtain a Presidential appointment to the Naval Academy and spent a year there before realising that it was not the life for him. He then tried the Army, entering the officers' training school in 1914 and finally receiving a regular commission as a second lieutenant of infantry in October 1917. While on leave, he married a local girl, and they had a son.

Bolling was posted to France with the 4th Infantry Division on 6 April 1918 in time to see action during the last six months of the Great War. He was wounded twice while taking part in the Aisne-Marne, Champagne-Marne and St Mihiel offensives. During this time, he was awarded the Distinguished Service Cross. The citation read: 'While in command of three widely separated platoons in the Bois-des-Nesles, on the night of 14th July 1918, Lieutenant Bolling continually exposed himself to very heavy gas and shell fire by going from one platoon to another.'

After World War One, Bolling remained in the Army as a regular officer. His peacetime career was successful and he gradually gained promotion through a series of administrative posts until he achieved his first star (brigadier-general) in March 1942. In June 1944, he took over the active command of the 84th Division.

Bolling was over six feet tall, slim, fit and always immaculately turned out. He was a friendly, personable man, well liked by his men, with a lively sense of humour. He wore spectacles, which gave him the appearance of a college professor, but there was nothing stuffy about him. By his own admission, he had collected nineteen reprimands during his army career, for a series of minor infringements of army rules. He always believed in action and took chances when he thought the risk justified it. Inevitably, this sometimes offended his superiors.

It is interesting to note that when Bolling took his division overseas into action, he was still only a brigadier-general. In fact, he was the only substantive brigadier-general commanding a front line division in the American Army. He did not get his second star until February 1945. Perhaps his nineteen reprimands held him back.

General Bolling was a devoutly religious man. The last thing he did before retiring each night, even on the battlefield, was to take communion with the divisional chaplain.

The 'Railsplitters' had a good general in command to lead them into battle. His experiences of the futility of World War One had shaped his attitude towards the taking of casualties. He was determined to keep losses to a minimum. The responsibility for each of his men who died was etched in his memory. After the war, Bolling kept a small piece of folded paper in his wallet and carried it with him at all times. On it was written a number. It was the total number of men killed in the 84th Division during the war.

If the 84th Division was led by a married, well respected career general, the British 43rd (Wessex) Division, in contrast, was led by an enigma. Horrocks described the 43rd's Commander as 'a very difficult man'. Indeed, a recent historian cites him as being, 'one of the most detested generals in the British Army', although perhaps this is going a bit too far. Undoubtedly, Thomas did have his detractors, for his prickly personality won him few friends. There was none of the personal charm of Horrocks about him, nor the sharp intellect and subtle humour of Montgomery. His blunt manner was hardly likely to win him any bouquets and his quick temper often put his subordinates in great fear of his wrath, but there was in him a quality that triumphed over all of his shortcomings, a quality that was fortunately recognised by his superiors: he was a true professional in an army that, in the main, consisted of gifted amateurs. In 1944, on the battlefields of Europe, that quality was just what the British Army needed.

Major-General Gwilym Ivor Thomas had been born on 23 July 1893 into a middle class musical family. His father was Master of the Queen's Music to Queen Victoria. Thomas was educated at Cheltenham College and the Royal Military Academy, Woolwich. At the age of nineteen, on 20 December 1912, he obtained a commission into the Royal Regiment of Artillery.

Three years later, just after the outbreak of war, he crossed over to France with the British Expeditionary Force. For the next three years he fought on the Western Front, seeing action in many of the bitter campaigns that took such a toll of human lives. Thomas was twice wounded, the second time badly enough to earn repatriation. By this time, he had been decorated three times for gallantry, winning the Distinguished Service Order, and the Military Cross and Bar, and had been mentioned in Dispatches.

After World War One, when he had recovered from his wounds, he became a student at the Staff College, Camberley and later at the Royal Naval Staff College. Thomas was to serve in various staff posts of increasing importance during the inter-war years until, in 1937, he took an appointment at the War Office. By October 1941, he had risen to the rank of major-general and was Commander Royal Artillery Home Forces. On 2 March 1942 he was given the command of the 43rd Infantry Division.

By 1942 Thomas had been a regular soldier for thirty years. He was forty-nine years old. He had had no life other than the Army. All his energy and effort had been directed towards this one career. He had by then developed a quite brilliant military mind, but his difficult personality had left him with few close friends. He was somewhat of a loner and kept himself withdrawn from everything. Thomas tended to model himself on Montgomery, whom he idolised, being similar to his chief in many ways. He had the same sort of crisp and aloof manner, a scowling and curt expression when displeased and, ironically, trouble pronouncing his 'r's. But Thomas had none of Montgomery's flair for self-publicity. Although very competent, he was in effect, a rather nondescript, middle-aged general.

Early in 1944 Thomas was having a little difficulty with the organisational ability of his aide-de-camp. This reached a climax when the unfortunate junior officer failed to book a sleeper for his master on the overnight train to

Edinburgh. Thomas was forced to endure an uncomfortable journey all the way to Scotland. The ADC was consequently sacked. To fill the vacant post, the War Office soon found the General a replacement in the person of Evelyn Waugh.

Waugh had applied to the War Office for leave to complete his latest novel – *Brideshead Revisited* – but was told that he had been found employment with Major-General Thomas as an ADC. At a meeting arranged over lunch at the Aperitif Restaurant in London, Waugh tried to warn Thomas that he was not the ideal man to be an aide-de-camp, but nonetheless the general was rather taken with the thought of having a literary celebrity on his staff and accepted the novelist for a week's trial.

It was a disaster. Waugh arrived at the Divisional HQ on Tuesday, 29 February, and was gone by the Thursday of the same week. The reason for his short stay and his relations with the general were recorded in Waugh's diary:

> The primary lack of sympathy seemed to come from my being slightly drunk in his mess on the first evening. I told him I could not change the habits of a lifetime for a whim of his. The HQ was architecturally deplorable and the staff glum and drab.

One of the staff officers at the HQ, Lieutenant-Colonel Williams Thomas, remembers Waugh's short stay and a quite different reason for his departure:

> Evelyn Waugh was always pretty well 'oiled' and got sacked shortly after his arrival when he came gangling down the stairs in 'A' Mess singing, 'His father was a harpist, his father was a harpist.' Waugh had been checking in *Who's Who* and discovered that Thomas's father had been a harpist to Queen Victoria. We all thought it was hilarious. I do not think Waugh was ever forgiven for letting the cat out of the bag!

The two days spent by Waugh at the Divisional HQ were long enough for him to change his mind completely concerning his opinion of Thomas. On their first meeting, Waugh described the general as, 'a very good little chap'. Later, he described him as, 'a man of insatiable ambition and unscrupulous in his means of self advancement.'

All this might lead to the opinion that Thomas was a bad general. In fact, the opposite was true. Thomas was regarded very favourably by his masters; he fought his division well. During the campaign in North-West Europe from June 1944 to May 1945, the 43rd Division suffered more casualties than any other, a total of 12,482, but it had been given some of the most difficult tasks of the campaign and it came through with honour. The division was always in the thick of the action, with its commander at its head.

The US 84th Division had been assigned to General Simpson's newly activated Ninth Army and was needed for the next 'big push'. It was scheduled to land at Cherbourg in France, but was diverted to Britain because the port was choked with shipping trying to unload. Some of the ships carrying the 84th berthed in Scotland, while the faster vessels were brought around southern England to be landed in Southampton.

Captain George Felton was aboard the SS *E.B. Alexander* which dropped anchor near Greenock, on the Firth of Clyde.

> The harbour was full of ships, including the *Queen Elizabeth* and the *Queen Mary*. We were all fascinated and kept looking at everything through our field glasses. There were people walking around and a few cars to be seen. It was a most beautiful day, and I can remember how we were all sure that anyone who would want to destroy such a beautiful country must be a fiend.

Once ashore, all the troops were loaded onto trains and the long journey south began. For most, it was the first foreign country that they had ever seen. They watched each town pass by with intense interest. Spirits were high. At night, when the blackout curtains were drawn, they knew that it really meant something. The war was drawing closer and closer.

Company G, of the 333rd Regiment, was dumped out on a cold windy hill a few miles outside Newbury, Berkshire. The men spent a few nights in a tented camp alongside Greenham Common airfield. Captain Felton was told that on the night before D-Day, General Eisenhower watched the US paratroops take off for the invasion from this airfield.

Further south, the 334th Regiment set up camp around the city of Winchester, the ancient capital of Wessex. Some units were billeted in the barracks of the Hampshire Regiment in the heart of the city. One battalion of the Hampshire Regiment, the 7th, was at that moment fighting with the British 43rd Division, in an effort to relieve the besieged paratroopers at Arnhem. Two months later, the 334th Regiment would eventually find itself joining the Hampshires in the mutual struggle against the Siegfried Line in Germany.

Although housed in solid brick buildings, there was nothing cosy about being in 'olde England'. Life for a soldier could still be rather miserable. 'We were cold in Winchester', recalls George Green from Company E of the 334th Regiment. 'We were billeted in the old barracks near the centre of the town. They only had outside shower stalls with cold water. At night, we slept on straw ticks and the wind whistled up through the floor. We went to bed in our long johns, shirt, trousers, overcoat and blanket, and still we lay there and shivered.'

If the camp life was rather primitive for the Americans, there was little comfort to be found in the night life of the cathedral city. Apart from the pubs, and a single dance hall, there was nothing. There was, however, some consolation to be had in the fact that the nation's capital was fairly near.

Some 'Railsplitters' did get to London on leave and managed to visit all the tourist sites. George Green took in a very sedate type of girlie show:

> I managed to see the 'Phyllis Dixie Revue Show'. I think the theatre was called The Windmill. Under English law, the girls were not required to wear too many adornments, but all they could do was pose, they were not allowed to move around. This was in stark contrast to the relatively rowdy American burlesque show dancing, but it was still very entertaining.

Those Americans that did get to London on furlough experienced the latest of Hitler's terror weapons – the V rockets. The V-1s, and the more powerful V-2s, fell indiscriminately throughout the city, finding mostly civilian targets. 'The buzz bombs came over from time to time', recalled George Green, who experienced several of these raids while he was there. 'You could hear this loud roar in the sky like a freight train coming. Then there would be a momentary silence, followed by an enormous explosion. Sometimes a whole city block would disappear into a pile of rubble, and all the while people just went about their normal business as though it was an everyday occurrence.'

Gil Bradham remembers his short stay in England:

> After spending a few uncomfortable days in a 'tent city' somewhere in Scotland, we were billeted in an army camp near Andover in Hampshire for about two weeks. I remember going to a local dance one night, which was my first chance to meet the local British people. I must say they were very nice and were concerned for our well being. I also paid a visit to Salisbury and had a look at the cathedral; an impressive sight for an untravelled country boy having just turned nineteen.

England was different from the USA, there was no doubt about that. The 334th Regiment's history sums up some of the contrasts:

> There was weak, warm beer instead of a Budweiser, bread pudding instead of ice cream, and left side of the road driving that left service companies in continuous apprehension. The people were shy but friendly. Everyone wore a uniform and, in contrast to the States, service seemed neither dramatic nor unique.

One month after arriving in England, the 'Railsplitters' were on the move again, this time to France. The time had come for them to join in the war.

The division landed in France on Omaha Beach. The ships carrying it over the Channel pulled to within about a mile of the shore before transferring the troops down rope ladders onto landing craft. The way that the tiny boats were tossed about by the heavy swell, made the move a little dangerous, but no one was seriously hurt. Once the small craft had a full load of men jammed onto the open decks, they headed for shore and the famous beach. The sense of history was lost on some, for many of the GIs were soon green with seasickness. Then, with a powerful jerk, they hit the sand.

Omaha Beach, France! The 'Railsplitters' had finally arrived on the continent of Europe.

There was debris everywhere. Wrecked ships littered the shoreline and gave witness to the fateful battle that had taken place there on 6 June. The troops had seen it all on the newsreels and they eagerly looked around for further signs of conflict.

Once ashore, the troops marched to a tented staging area. From there they were later bussed across France and Belgium into Holland towards the front line. Eventually they crossed the German border and into battle.

In contrast to the 84th Division's leisurely passage across Europe into Germany, the British 43rd (Wessex) Division had to fight for almost every mile of the way. The Wessexmen had originally, like the 'Railsplitters', landed on the D-Day beaches, but some four months previously on 22 June. The Division's first action had been in a supporting role during the advance on the Odon river.

The 43rd Division's first full-scale attack was against the strong German positions on top of the infamous Hill 112. It was a terrible affair; over two thousand casualties were suffered by the division during the battle. Then came the rest of the bloody Normandy campaign. The Wessex Division took part in most of the major battles in the lodgement area, including the capture of Mont Pinçon.

After the breakout, the division executed a famous one hundred mile advance across France which culminated in the brilliant assault crossing of the River Seine at Vernon. This epic operation opened the door to XXX Corps' lightning armoured dash across northern France and Belgium. The next battle was the Arnhem affair 'the bridge too far'. The 43rd was the part of XXX Corps' relief column which tried to join up with the besieged paratroopers in Arnhem itself. The division met with the most ferocious German opposition imaginable, between the Waal and Neder Rhine rivers. Historians have always been very critical of the part played by the division in the Arnhem offensive. The true story of what really happened has yet to be told.

After the Arnhem battle, came a spell holding the front line around Nijmegen. Then the move south into Germany was announced; the division was posted into the line at Geilenkirchen.

Chapter Three

Into the Line

XXX Corps' proposed attack on the Geilenkirchen salient had been given the codename Operation Clipper. The battle was planned to develop through four phases. First, a regiment of the 84th Division was to attack through the line held by the US 102nd Division and take Prummern and the high ground to the east of Geilenkirchen. Second, about five hours after the start of this attack, the British 43rd Division was to assault the villages to the west of the town and cut the road leading into it from the north-east. These two attacks would virtually encircle Geilenkirchen. Thereupon, a second regiment of the 84th would carry out the third phase of the operation and strike the town head on from the south. In the final phase of the operation, the two divisions would advance along both sides of the Wurm valley and clear the villages to the north of Geilenkirchen as far as Wurm.

The successful conclusion of Clipper would eliminate the salient between the British and American boundary and secure the Ninth US Army's left flank during its advance to the River Roer. This final boundary would follow the course of the River Wurm from Geilenkirchen and then swing north-eastwards along the line of the railway to Mönchengladbach. Once the operation was completed, no further attacks were planned for XXX Corps. The next major offensive for the British was to be Montgomery's drive eastwards from Nijmegen in Holland.

D Day for Operation Clipper was set for Saturday, 18 November. This was two days after the start of General Bradley's main offensive, Operation Queen, had kicked off. The Ninth US Army's part in that operation was to attack through the Westwall to the line of the River Roer with its XIX Corps, consisting of the 2nd Armored and the 29th and 30th Infantry Divisions.

The American 2nd Armored Division was on Ninth Army's left flank next to the British XXX Corps. Its objective was to take the town of Gereonsweiler and the high ground to the north. Simpson then intended to introduce his XIII Corps into the battle. The 102nd Infantry Division was to pass through the 2nd Armored and push on towards the River Roer. By then, the operation to clear

Geilenkirchen should be completed and the 84th Division could be returned to XIII Corps, to close on the Roer.

For its part in Operation Queen, the 30th Division was given the 335th Regiment from the 84th Division. The attachment took place on 9 November and was to last for several weeks. In consequence, the 335th took no part in Operation Clipper and the capture of Geilenkirchen.

Once it had finally arrived in Germany, the US 84th Division went into the line in a defensive capacity. Together with the newly arrived 102nd Infantry Division, the 'Railsplitters' took over the responsibility of the sector around Geilenkirchen. Their task was to hold the front and gather as much information about the enemy as possible. These duties enabled the two new divisions to be introduced gradually to battle conditions, before going into offensive action.

Prior to moving up to the front line to relieve the 2nd Armored Division, the 405th Regiment of the 102nd Division was in training near Maastricht in Holland. Bob Enkelmann was a forward observer with the heavy weapons company. The night before his company was due to move out, Enkelmann was with a few members of his squad being briefed by his sergeant:

All of us had dug our first foxholes; they were so deep that you needed a ladder to get out. Our sergeant, an old army man, had the job of briefing us. The squad consisted of a mixture of illiterates and men with high IQs. His talk was on the lines of; 'This is it men,' and 'Write your last letters to your mothers/sisters/girlfriends,' together with other such encouraging information. He had been drinking. We could always tell when he had been drinking, because he would be devoid of his bridge, usually because he had become sick and flushed his dentures down the latrine. While he was talking, we heard the sound of what we thought was a malfunctioning washing machine, but paid no attention to it. Had we been in receipt of a bit of combat experience, we might have realised it was one of Herman Goering's finest, with a tank of ersatz petrol, hunting for our neighbouring ammunition dump on which to unload its bombs. When the plane had finally found it, the sound of the bombs dropping and the resulting concussions from the munitions exploding, sent us all diving for the nearest foxhole to escape certain death. Needless to say, it belonged to our beloved sergeant and we all piled in on top of him, in a sardinelike fashion. He blew his top and ran around threatening to have us all courtmartialled and sent home, until he realised that that was our most fervent hope at that moment.

The 102nd Division went into the line on 23 October, relieving infantry components of the 2nd Armored Division. Frank Mead was with the 405th Regiment and he painfully remembers the conditions:

The weather was terrible; almost constant freezing rain with occasional sleet. The terrain was flat and, while it gave excellent visibility, gave no natural protective cover. In front of us, the Krauts had produced a number of formidable obstacles in the form of anti-tank ditches and trenches. The constant rain and overcast skies seemed to prevent any evaporation. The earth was just plain mud. Our foxholes were virtual wells and the anti-tank ditches stagnant canals. No matter how careful we were, our weapons became constantly clogged and jammed by the mud. It was combat under the worst possible conditions.

Once in the line, the 84th Division also took on a defensive role watching the front. There was little activity, save for patrolling and an occasional enemy shelling. Gil Bradham was a private with 333rd Regiment's Company C:

There was virtually no action taking place in that area, we were just outpost guards. We were quite thinly stretched on the ground, our foxholes were about 150 yards apart. The nights were long and the only action we experienced was an occasional burst of 'burp' gun fire from the Germans, just to let us know they were still there. I happened to get paired with an older regular army type, he was maybe thirty three. One night, being younger than him and respecting his age, I offered to take the first watch. I did my stint and stayed on as long as I could keep my eyes open. Finally I woke this guy up and handed over the watch to him. Some time later, I awoke and found that he had fallen asleep. I was as mad as hell. I forgot my manners and abruptly woke him up, making him a promise that if he ever did that again, I would make sure that he would never wake up!

When, on 12 November, the British XXX Corps moved south from Nijmegen to take up its new positions between Geilenkirchen and the River Maas, the front line there was being held by elements of the US 113th Cavalry Group, the 84th Division and the 102nd Division. The Guards Armoured Division took over the northern section, while the 43rd Division occupied the sector that had been held by the American 102nd Division.

General Thomas, of the 43rd Division, had already decided that he would mount his coming attack to the east of Geilenkirchen with the whole of 214 Brigade, reinforced with a battalion from 130 Brigade. Therefore, he put 129 Brigade into the line and kept the remaining two battalions of 130 Brigade in reserve.

The British 129 Brigade relieved the American 407th Regiment of its responsibility of holding the front line on 11 November. Its commander, Brigadier Mole, established his headquarters just north of Brunssum, right on

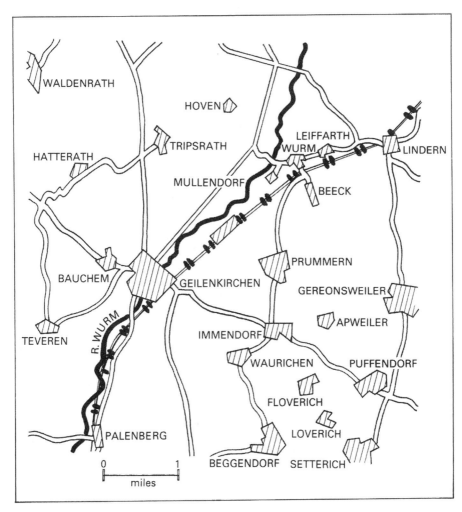

Map 2: The Geilenkirchen Area.

the Dutch-German border. A few miles away, inside Germany, Lieutenant Colonel Michael Concannon set out the 25 pounder field guns of the 94th Field Regiment Royal Artillery. It was an historic occasion; for the first time since the battle of Minden in 1759, British guns were being laid for action on German soil.

The handing over of the line went very smoothly, with little fire being drawn from the enemy positions. There was some light-hearted banter between the British and American troops, each side picking on the other's eccentricities, but in general, the 407th was glad to be out of the line, while 129 Brigade was pleased to be taking over such a quiet spot after all its recent fighting.

The Americans had left minefields in front of all their positions. When the British took over, little was known about their exact location. General Thomas quite rightly anticipated that these minefields would cause problems for 214 Brigade when it made its attack. Consequently, he ordered the mines to be lifted. Fourteen hundred mines were removed before the area was deemed to be clear.

The mines were collected by 204 Field Company Royal Engineers and were then taken back to the rear. A dump was arranged near the Custom House on the Dutch border, right next to 129 Brigade's Headquarters.

On the morning of 14 November, Brigadier Mole carried out his tour of the line as usual. Normally his gunner, Lieutenant-Colonel Concannon, accompanied him, but that morning the Brigadier said he would go alone. On returning, Mole noticed the unusual activity going on alongside his headquarters and went over to talk to the Royal Engineer officer in charge of the work. As he approached, something went horribly wrong. Hundreds of the mines exploded with an almightly roar. The explosion blew a crater thirty feet across.

Concannon was quickly on the scene, but it was too late. 'I found the Brigadier still alive, but badly wounded. There were bodies everywhere. Parts of limbs could be seen hanging from the trees.' Fourteen sappers were killed in the blast and six others seriously wounded. Brigadier Mole was taken back to a field hospital in Brunssum. He died later that day.

It was a sad loss for the Wessex Division. Brigadier Mole was a brilliant commander. He had led his brigade through some of the worst fighting of the whole war. His battle honours were many. He was laid to rest in a cemetery in Brunssum. As the buglers of the 4th Somerset Light Infantry sounded the 'Last Post' over his grave, Concannon's 94th Field Regiment fired a final salute to its dead commander, directed, as he would have wished, against targets in the enemy's lines.

Whenever the British and American forces came into contact with each other, alongside the obvious mutual respect for each other's role in the war, there was always a touch of xenophobia. The British soldier's way of doing things was not quite the same as that of his American allies and vice versa. Private Arthur Hitchcock was in 129 Brigade, with the 4th Somerset Light Infantry and recalls the changeover:

We took over from the Americans and a very green lot they were too. They had not seen much action and seemed to be always walking around in the open in broad daylight. At night when we sent out our patrols, we set the whole place alight walking into trip wires they had set out with flares attached. There was one consolation though, some of the fox holes we took over were like a king's larders; the food they left behind pepped our spirits up!

Another of 129 Brigade's battalions was the 4th Wiltshires. Commanding C Company was Major Derek 'Dim' Robbins. His company took over the occupation of a village called Hatterath from the Americans. The positions were some of the most exposed of the entire front line. The village protruded well into enemy territory and formed a slim salient into an open area of field. Major Robbins remembers the scene:

> Hatterath was an eerie place. It was very, very quiet. It was pinpointed out into the enemy lines, completely deserted, a 'one horse' town. All the houses had good strong cellars. We felt comparatively safe in these cellars when the shells came in. However, outside the village we had to have forward platoons in forward positions. These were very important to us, for that is where the information came from about the enemy. Our task in Hatterath was to probe into the German lines and find out their positions and minefields. We had to do a lot of patrolling. I also pushed small listening posts hundreds of yards out in front of our lines, into enemy territory to monitor his movements. These were manned by very brave chaps, lance-corporals most of them, out on their own in no-mans-land. Quite often, German patrols would pass within feet of their hides without discovering them.

As the Americans gave up their section of the front line, so they relinquished the villages in the rear to the control of the British. Many of the buildings and facilities used by the Americans were now taken over by the Wessex Division. The new owners were amazed to find that the local inhabitants were still in occupation. The British did not share the Americans' ambivalent attitude towards German civilians. The troops were not sure that the local population could be relied on to refrain from passing on information to their countrymen, just a few miles away across the front line. Within a short space of time, it was made clear to the villagers that there had been *another* change of management!

On the morning of 17 November, the day before Clipper began, seven British trucks arrived in the straggling village of Grotenrath, three miles to the south of Geilenkirchen. All of the 170 people who were living in the village were rounded up by military police and ordered to bring a few of their personal belongings with them to the trucks parked in the square in Walderstrasse. The British were evacuating all German civilians from the village. By noon the lorries had been loaded and had left for Holland, destination Vught.

Brigadier Hubert Essame, Commander of 214 Brigade, had little sympathy for the plight of the German civilians. As he explained later in the divisional history: 'At long last the Germans were being paid in their own coin. For years they had brought misery such as this to the other peoples of Europe. Now they realised for the first time what it meant to be a refugee, homeless, drifting nowhere in the November rain.'

The camp at Vught had once been a German concentration camp. Liberated by the Allies, it had been put back into commission as a containment area for German civilians. It was guarded and policed by the Dutch. Little compassion was shown to these Germans who suddenly found themselves the innocent victims of a brutal war. Although their fate was not as cruel as that of previous inmates, seven of those taken from Grotenrath died in captivity at the camp.

Some people from Grotenrath managed to escape the British roundup. Agnes Schummertz, her mother and her sister succeeded in getting to the next village of Scherpenseel. That village was still in the American zone and they were able to remain there. A little later, Agnes returned to Grotenrath to see what had become of her home and their animals. The British were using their 'gasthaus', or inn, as a headquarters building. The animals had all been slaughtered. When she asked about the dead animals she was told, 'ah, that was the Americans'.

Prior to the British taking over the village of Grotenrath, Agnes Schummertz had made friends with a young American soldier who was acting in the dual role of interpreter for General Bolling and administrator to the German civilians. His name was Henry Kissinger.

Henry Kissinger was born in Germany. His family had fled the Nazi persecution of the Jews in 1937 and had settled in the USA. Heinz (he later changed his name to Henry) was brought up as an American. Quite naturally, when he became of age, he was drafted into the American army. His high IQ enabled him to be accepted for the ASTP and he was sent to college. With the demise of the programme, he found himself posted to the 84th Division where he had the good fortune to meet an extraordinary private called Kraemer.

Fritz Kraemer was a German intellectual who had also left his homeland because of the Nazis. Unlike Kissinger, he was a Protestant, a devout Christian who regarded Naziism as an abhorrence. After the Japanese attack on Pearl Harbor and America's entry into the war, he enlisted in the Army. Kraemer's German background and high intellect resulted in him being given the job of educating the officers and men of the 84th Division on the subject of military government and political affairs. The impact of Kissinger's meeting with Kraemer was profound.

Kissinger was overwhelmed by the well-educated European, thirteen years his senior, and learned much from his contact with him. The young Kissinger became aware of his own serious academic limitations and sought to improve his mind through Kraemer. In return, Kraemer was impressed with the young Jew. 'I saw in him a man of discipline and initiative,' Kraemer was later to recall. 'He knew nothing and yet understood everything.' Henry Kissinger became his protégé.

Private Fritz Kraemer had the ear of General Bolling and arranged for Kissinger to take up the post of German-speaking interpreter for the 84th Division's Commander. It was the beginning of a career that led to great things. After the war, he remained in Germany as an administrator of the district of Bergstrasse. His accomplishments impressed Kraemer, who in turn spoke complimentarily of him to Bolling. Kissinger soon rose to sergeant and was transferred to the European Command Intelligence School. On his return to the USA, he enrolled at Harvard University. The rest is history. This young German-American 'Railsplitter', who saw his first action as a private at Geilenkirchen, rose to be one of the twentieth century's great statesmen.

Chapter Four

Preparations for Battle

It was hoped that Operation Queen, General Bradley's joint First and Ninth Army offensive in the south, might draw away some of the German opposition around Geilenkirchen from the area. Operation Queen was to be launched two days earlier than Clipper, 16 November.

Opposite the British XXX Corps in the line was the German 183rd Volks Grenadier Division, commanded by Generalleutnant Wolfgang Lange. The 183rd Division had been re-activated during the first half of September 1944, after having been virtually eliminated during the fighting in Russia. It was composed of remnants of headquarters and other staffs of the Corps Detachment C. Fifty-one per cent of the divisional personnel were Austrians, the majority from the Lower Danube and Vienna. Many of the enlisted men had been deferred for years. Very little time was allotted to it for training and Lange was critical of the decision to send it into the line without having exercised at all with combined-arms units.

The activation period was fourteen days. After that, the division was transported to the Western Front. As the various units arrived, they took up positions on both sides of Geilenkirchen during the latter part of September. They arrived in time to bolster the German defence of the area and halt the American advance. The division was responsible for a front of just over ten miles, stretching from Birgden, through Geilenkirchen to Ubach. To the south was the German 49th Infantry Division, and to the north, the 176th Infantry Division. Both of these divisions had already been badly mauled by the Americans. During the slight lull that followed, defences in the area were improved, especially around the Siegfried Line emplacements where additional trenches and anti-tank ditches were dug.

On 2 October the American 30th Infantry Division had attacked in the direction Ubach-Palenberg. The assault hit the boundary between the German 183rd Division and the 49th Division. 'From some of our advanced observation posts one could see, and almost count, the overwhelming number of attacking tanks and forces that followed them,' recalled General Lange after the war. 'By evening, about eighty American tanks had crossed the River Wurm. Ubach-Palenberg was lost.'

The German division counter attacked early on 3 October, but regained little ground. This new American attack prompted the German LXXXI Corps Commander, General Koechling, to reinforce Lange's 183rd Division with men from the NCO Training Schools, Dueren and Juelich. These new troops had been expected to arrive in the area to relieve the 183rd Division's 343rd Grenadier Regiment in Geilenkirchen, so that it could be used in a concerted attack against the Americans. Unfortunately for Lange, these reinforcements arrived too late to be of any real help and were fed into the line piecemeal.

The attachment of these specialist troops from the two NCO Training schools to an infantry division was evidence of the crisis facing the German Army at that time. Manpower, throughout the whole of the country, was in very short supply. Lange was again highly critical of his higher command for using these skilled men in this way:

> Although the subordination of these units improved the combat value of the division for a short time, the use at the front of such first rate units as one body must be condemned. Their organisation, armament and equipment were not quite sufficient for employment at the front. They were in some respects lacking, and in others abundant. It meant wasting first rate personnel without receiving adequate profit. If the two NCO schools had been immediately distributed over the entire division, its combat value would have been improved considerably, and could have been maintained at a higher level. The employment of the schools as separate units resulted in high losses, and later, when they were both finally distributed to the entire army group, no unit profited perceptibly.

The American offensive went on for five more days but, although it managed to widen the penetration, it could not achieve a breakthrough. The front reverted to stalemate once again and the line remained static for the next four weeks. Both armies were able to consolidate their positions with little opposition.

The situation along the front line then settled down into a monotonous round of daily routines. Each side shelled the other intermittently, sent out patrols and sniped at anyone foolish enough to show themselves. The infantry on both sides had gone to ground. Life was lived out of holes dug in the wet earth. Along the whole of the sector, one line of American trenches looked out across open ground to another line of German dug outs. Shadows of the Great War had returned to the battlefields of Europe.

Bob Enkelmann was a forward observer with the 3rd Battalion's heavy weapon company. It was his job to control the firing of the heavy mortars. One morning he was sent up to a captured pillbox on a hill overlooking

Geilenkirchen. The bunker contained a rifle platoon leader and an artillery observer. The exposed route out to the surveillance post took him up a hill and along a ridge. All the way up to the post, he prayed that the enemy would not start shelling the ridge before he had gained entry to the pillbox. He made it safely to the bunker and stepped inside to find one very incensed officer.

> Lieutenant Kaiser had been peering through his scope and had spotted a Kraut digging a foxhole near a fence at the edge of the town, blatantly ignoring the fact that he was being watched. Kaiser became so furious that he called for artillery fire to be brought down on the unfortunate German. The artillery commander politely informed him that they were conserving ammunition and they could not fire a barrage on anything less than a squad. Kaiser then turned to me and asked me to drop a few shells on the Kraut. This was my first big chance. I passed the co-ordinates back to my 80mm mortars and asked for a smoke shell. It landed several hundred feet over target. I adjusted and asked for another; that landed several hundred feet short. I again corrected and asked for a barrage to be fired. To my amazement, the mortar shells landed even further away in Geilenkirchen. Exasperated, Kaiser said, 'To hell with you, we'll try to get him with our own mortars.' Damned me if they didn't drop a round directly into the hole that the German was digging. I later found out that one of our practising illiterates, who had claimed he had memorised the firing chart, was our gunner that day!

Geilenkirchen was a small town situated astride the River Wurm. It was a communications centre, with good road and rail connections. The peacetime population was around twenty thousand inhabitants, but by November 1944 its population had been reduced to zero. All the civilians had been evacuated months before. Geilenkirchen had become a battle zone; heavily fortified by the military, it had been incorporated into the Siegfried Line.

The terrain around the town was dominated by the River Wurm, although 'river' might be considered too grand a word for what amounted to no more than a slender stream about twenty feet wide. On the right of the river was a section of high ground that stretched up to a large, fairly flat plateau, before descending once again to meet the River Roer, about six miles away. This was the area alloted to the US 84th Division during the coming battle. On the left of the river, the side allocated to the British 43rd Division, the area was mostly flat farmland, studded with the occasional dense wood.

The Siegfried Line at this point generally followed the line of the River Wurm, with the most dense concentration of emplacements on the American side, especially along the high ground overlooking the river. It was one of the strongest sections of the entire Westwall. The town of Geilenkirchen acted as a bastion, guarding the point where the line swung north-eastwards along the valley. With such a perfect defensive line confronting them, it was difficult to decide who had the hardest task in the operation: the British who would have to attack under the eyes of the guns on the high ground; or the Americans who would have to clear the fortifications from close quarters.

The open countryside, thick with crops of sugar beet and cabbage, afforded uncluttered observation and fields of fire from the German defences. There were very few means of concealment for any attacking troops. The enemy had created his strongpoints around the scattered villages of the area. Each one was linked together with its neighbour by earthworks and concrete pillboxes. Between them were hundreds of yards of perfectly open ground.

There were several types of pillboxes in use: machine gun, anti-tank, personnel and headquarters bunkers. They each varied in size according to their role. The smallest held six men, while the personnel bunkers held up to forty men. The walls were a minimum of three feet thick. Some had up to seven feet of reinforced concrete to protect those inside.

The siting of these emplacements was near perfect. The enemy had had a long time to consider all avenues of approach. He cleverly utilised the natural features of the area and merged his pillboxes into the existing terrain. Earth was piled on top and around some of the emplacements to help to camouflage them. All of them were protected by interlocking fields of fire and reinforced by minefields, barbed wire and trenches.

Rivers and streams were converted into anti-tank ditches by widening their beds and straightening their banks. Concrete and steel 'dragon's teeth' obstacles were laid for miles across the hillsides. All road intersections were covered by anti-tank emplacements.

It was not tank country. Armoured vehicles would be exposed at all times to the fire of anti-tank guns. Nor was it infantry country. The unconcealed riflemen could be seen coming miles away. In fact, it was no place to be fighting a war in at all. But then, the Wessexmen and the 'Railsplitters' had no say in the matter.

As the day approached for the start of Operation Clipper, so the pace of preparations began to increase. For the British 43rd Division it was just one more attack. For the US 84th Division, it was its first. Both divisions saw things differently; the American way of doing things was certainly not the British way.

The 84th Division was immaculately turned out, with each man intent on doing his duty, exactly as he had been told during training. Just one day of battle on the Siegfried Line would change all that, but in the meantime, everyone followed regulations.

One would expect that the innate conservatism of the British would also show itself in an attitude of 'correctness and propriety'. In fact, the opposite is true. By this time in the war, the 43rd Division had seen too much action to stand on ceremony. The officers dressed as they pleased, often in flamboyant style, with silk scarves and leather jackets. Although the British Army traditionally always 'went by the book', the book was, occasionally, overlooked in favour of convenience and experience. In some ways the British felt superior to the new arrivals, for there was the inevitable condescension that is present when fighting men, who have won their spurs in action, are confronted by green troops. Most of the British had some amusing comments to make about their American cousins at the start of this battle. But later, when it was all over and the cost was counted, they had nothing but praise for them. The affinity that privation and courage forged between the soldiers of these two countries can still be found to this day.

Prior to the start of the battle, there was much communicating between the British and the Americans to make sure that everyone knew just what was expected of them. Lieutenant Pat Spencer Moore was the ADC to Major-General Thomas, Commander of the 43rd Division, and remembers attending a briefing at the American headquarters:

> There were five of us from the British side; General Thomas, Brigadier Boyland [Commander Royal Artillery], a gunner lieutenant, a corporal and myself. Confronting us were the American general, his deputy and a whole row of senior officers of descending rank, about a dozen in total. The object of the meeting was to explain the rolling barrage that was to be fired by the artillery in front of the infantry during the coming attack. Boyland handed proceedings over to the lieutenant and the corporal, who went on to outline the plan in detail. The Americans were amazed to find out that just this young lieutenant and a corporal would be running the show.

On another occasion Spencer Moore was at an American 'orders' group with the general, where details of the attack were made known to all the US commanders involved in the battle. General Thomas sat watching as the various tasks were explained. The boundaries between the American units were marked on the map with bold coloured lines. Thomas raised the question of whether the main axis road through that sector which formed one of the boundaries was inclusive, or exclusive, to the area assigned to the adjacent unit. The question caused a little uncertainty, for the point obviously had not been considered in precise detail. A spirited discussion followed between the Americans to try to decide one way or another. Spencer Moore recalls that the matter was still not precisely cleared up at that meeting by the time he and the general had left.

Other meetings took place as the various units sorted out details of the attack. Just before the battle, Brigadier Essame, Commander of the British 214 Brigade, asked Lieutenant-Colonel George Taylor, Commander 5th Duke of

Cornwall's Light Infantry, to go across to the Americans and make contact with the battalion commander who was to lead their attack. Taylor recalled:

I saw their colonel, a short dark haired man called Gomes. We fixed up various points of contact and co-operation, including the use of yellow smoke to show up our progress in the advance. As I was leaving him, having wished him good fortune in this his first battle, I made a throwaway remark saying, 'Don't put all your goods in the shop window.' He quickly responded and asked me what I meant. Without being too patronising, for he was many years my junior, I was able to advocate the use of depth in the attack. We had a thorough discussion in which he went into great detail and obviously took note of what I said. I heard later that his battalion fought a very successful battle.

Lieutenant-Colonel Taylor was happy to be working with the Americans of the 84th Division:

They had just arrived from the States and were a completely new formation. From what I saw, briefly, of their training, they looked excellent troops. Horrocks was determined to help them, for he knew that their first battle was going to be a difficult and tough one, and so he put the experienced Sherwood Rangers tanks under their command.

The Sherwood Rangers Yeomanry was one of the most experienced tank regiments of the British Army. It had had a long war, seeing action both in North Africa and Europe. The regiment had landed on the Normandy beaches on D-Day and had fought all the way up to the Siegfried Line. Horrocks now placed this crack armoured unit under the command of the Americans, to help them break through Hitler's Westwall.

The Sherwood Rangers were part of the British 8th Armoured Brigade. The other two regiments, the 4th/7th Royal Dragoon Guards and the 13th/18th Royal Hussars were to be employed on the British side of the battlefield. In addition, to help breach the fortifications of the Siegfried Line, Horrocks had the assistance of elements from the British 79th Armoured Division.

The British 79th Armoured Division was equipped with a strange collection of armoured vehicles, designed for all kinds of special tasks. It had flame throwing tanks, mine clearing flail tanks, assault tanks capable of firing 60 lb charges against concrete emplacements, bridging tanks, fascine tanks and so on. A selection of these 'funnies', under the command of Colonel Drew was assigned to XXX Corps for the duration of Operation Clipper.

The day before the battle started, Charles Hinds from the US 2nd Armored Division, who were next to XXX Corps in the line, was ordered into liaison duties with a British armoured unit. His armoured car arrived in front of the town at nightfall to find a line of tanks from the British 79th Armoured Division. He was not pleased with what he saw:

> The British tanks were bunched together, something which always drove us crazy to see. We had been trained by Patton to keep sufficient distance between tanks so that one enemy shell could not put two vehicles out of commission. Furthermore, the British were shining their flashlights around the tanks – again, something that we never did. When our officer returned from reporting to their headquarters, he had us back away from the bunched up British tanks. Fortunately, the Germans did not take advantage of this poor armour discipline.

Just before midday on 16 November 1944, the air above Geilenkirchen was filled with large numbers of heavy bombers. Two and a half thousand aircraft from the US Eighth Air Force and Royal Air Force Bomber Command bombed the German ground forces in front of the Allies. Operation Queen, General Bradley's great winter offensive, was under way. Forty-five minutes later, the American troops attacked.

Seventeen Allied divisions blasted their way forward all along the line. At the northern end, next to the British XXX Corps, the US 2nd Armored Division moved on Immendorf, supported by the 102nd Infantry Division. Hundreds of thousands of soldiers were in action that day, each one of them fighting his own little battle to survive.

Edwin Dojka was a private first class in Company F of the 406th Regiment of the 102nd Division. He remembers the equipment he carried into the attack: an M1 rifle, bayonet, cartridge belt with ten clips of ammunition, entrenching tool (folding hand shovel), canteen, first aid kit, raincoat and combat pack with one day's supply of K and D rations. He also carried two extra bandoliers of ammunition, a grenade pouch with six to eight grenades and finally, two bangalore torpedoes (two and a half inch diameter, five feet long pipes of explosives).

Dojka, along with five other members of his squad, was carrying the bangalore torpedoes to deal with a minefield that had been located just in front of the battalion's objective of Immendorf. The advance went according to plan and the squad stopped in front of the minefield. Two engineers from the 2nd Armored came up and began to assemble the torpedoes. They carried a five foot wooden dummy with a wooden cap that would serve as the lead section of the explosive line and would, hopefully, absorb the blast of a schu mine should one be set off accidentally.

Dojka and his squad proceeded to deliver the explosive pipes to the engineers who coupled them together and then pushed them through the minefield. They lit the fuse and quickly ran back ten yards and took cover in a shell hole. Nothing happened. About a minute later one of the engineers returned to re-light the fuse. Again, nothing happened. By this time, the delay was holding up the battalion's attack and the engineers suggested that Dojka and his companion fire their rifles into the torpedoes to set them off. Both of them fired a clip of eight rounds into the explosives. Still nothing. Then another two clips were fired and this time Dojka noticed a small puff of white smoke rising from the fuse end of the pipe. Then, suddenly, it exploded, though not in its entirety, for a portion of the pipe was blown into the air, then fell and exploded again, leaving a sizeable area of the minefield untouched.

Edwin Dojka's platoon then advanced through this incompletely cleared section of the minefield. Unfortunately, seven of the men did not make it safely through; as they stepped on a mine they lost a leg, or worse. The platoon aid man was later killed in the minefield while tending to the wounded. Company F carried on towards their objective and into Immendorf.

Immendorf was taken and held by the 102nd Infantry while the 2nd Armored Division continued the advance. It reached the outskirts of Gereonsweiler, but made little more progress.

Four separate enemy counter attacks were made over the next two days to recapture Immendorf. The German 9th Panzer Division, veterans of the Russian Front, and the 15th Panzer Grenadier Division, dispatched forty-five tanks, backed by infantry, against the Americans. Immendorf, and the line, held. The 2nd Armored Division had forced the Germans to commit some of their reserves against its assault. This would be of great help to XXX Corps when the attack on Geilenkirchen began. With Immendorf and the right flank now in safe hands, the way had been opened for Horrocks to begin his assault on time.

Situation at 2359 hours, Friday, 17 November
Operation Clipper was due to begin in seven hours time. Everything was set. The US 84th Division and the British 43rd Division were ready for action. For the Americans, it was to be their first taste of battle, an indoctrination into the art of war. For the British, it was to be a most satisfying moment: they had finally brought the war home to Germany itself.

The 2nd Armored Division's action on the right had drawn off some of the German reserves opposite XXX Corps. Intelligence suggested that facing the Corps was a single Volks Grenadier Division. The battle should not be too difficult.

Chapter Five

The Attack

Saturday, 18 November 1944, promised to be as dull and wet as most of the preceding days of that month had been. The depressing weather seemed appropriate for the battle – squalid weather to match the squalid, desolate landscape. It was somehow fitting that the inevitable death and destruction that was about to be unleashed should take place in such a sombre setting.

The gloomy backdrop more than matched the sober mood of the hundreds of young American infantrymen of the 334th Regiment assembling at the staging area in the coal mines of Palenberg, prior to the final move to the start line.

'We talked that night of how many of us would be alive the following night,' recalls Frank Pinto of Company A. 'Our regimental commander had promised us a sort of celebration in Prummern after the battle, but I was sceptical.'

The 334th Regiment of the American 84th Division was to open the battle. The first phase of the operation was to capture the right flank of the battlefield by taking the village of Prummern and the high ground that overlooked Geilenkirchen. With the eastern side thus secure, the British 43rd Division could, later on in the day, move against the left flank in the west.

The attack was to begin with a breakout from the static positions that had been held for the last few weeks. Immediately in front of the American lines at Briell was an enemy minefield. This would have to be breached before any offensive moves could begin. 'Drew Force', part of the specialised armour from the British 79th Armoured Division, was given the job of clearing two paths through the minefield an hour before the attack was due to begin. Two battalions of the 334th Regiment would then pass through these two gaps and make for the objectives; the 1st Battalion, on the right, would head for the village of Prummern, while the 2nd Battalion, on the left, would move to the strategically important high ground between the village and Geilenkirchen itself. Both battalions would be supported by a squadron of tanks from the British Sherwood Rangers Yeomanry. The regiment's third battalion was kept in reserve. 'H' Hour, the start of the battle, was set for 0700 hours.

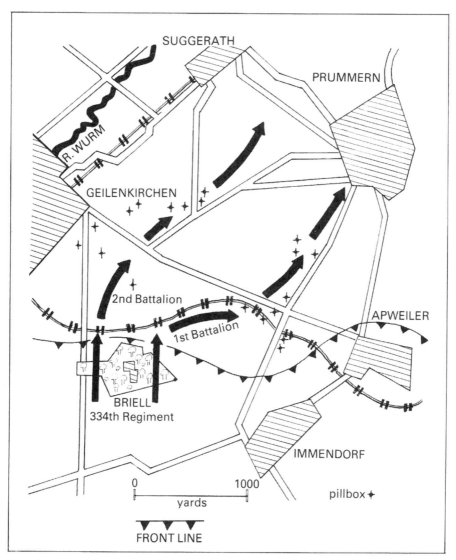

Map 3: The Attack by the 334th Regiment on Prummern.

At around 0300 hours, the first of the American infantry were roused from their sleep and ordered out into the cold damp air. Frank Pinto was one of those young soldiers in Palenberg that morning:

We were put into a coal mine as a staging area until it came time for us to go into the line. I remember coming out of the mine into the darkness and going through a mess line and getting what we thought was to be hot coffee, but which turned out to be a canteen cup of British rum. As a nineteen year old non-drinker I got quite a surprise on the first gulp.

The rum was part of the ration that was given to all British troops each day. As the US 84th Division was now part of the British XXX Corps, each man in the unit qualified for the ration. To most it was a very pleasant surprise, to some it was a less welcome ritual. Richard Howland was well aware of the consequences:

> We were offered the rum before we entered battle. Many of the older men, in their late twenties and thirties, took their ration, but some of the younger men – late teens, early twenties, declined and gave theirs to the older group. I am sure that the false bravado and recklessness of a significant number of those who took extra rations resulted in excessive casualties. I was deeply affected by this.

At 0400 hours, the first group of infantry left the coal mine and set off across the empty fields to the forming-up point in the tiny village of Hoverhof. Their initiation to combat was just two short hours away.

Breaching teams, from the 1st Lothian and Borderers' Yeomanry, had been instructed to make two gaps through the minefield in front of the small hamlet of Briell. This specialised armoured regiment was equipped with Sherman Crab mine clearing tanks. The Sherman Crab used giant flailing chains attached to a powered rotor to beat the ground, exploding mines as it rolled forward. It was able to clear a safe path ten feet wide at a speed of one and a half miles per hour.

The left, or Blue, gap was about a hundred yards to the right of the Geilenkirchen-Ubach road. The right, or Red, gap, was in front of the Geilenkirchen-Immendorf railway at a point where it crossed the road to Waurichen. This railway cut across the line of attack at right angles. Enemy infantry were known to be dug in along the railway embankment.

Clearing an enemy minefield is a very difficult task. Clearing an enemy minefield at night is doubly so. Any direct lighting of the area is sure to bring down enemy counter fire. Moonlight was a help, but the damp, cloudy nights of November held out little hope of assistance from that quarter. However, the British had been experimenting for a long time with the generation of 'artificial moonlight' as a means of giving some illumination to night operations. It was produced by shining powerful searchlights onto the base of low clouds. Some of this light was reflected down again to earth, producing sufficient brightness to assist troops on the ground. At Geilenkirchen, the 357th Searchlight Battery Royal Artillery was assigned to provide this 'artificial moonlight'.

Red column were on the forming-up point at 0530 hours and moved off on schedule at 0600 hours. One of the 1st Lothian and Borderers' flail tanks failed to cross the start line, having broken down, leaving Number 2 Troop with just three tanks with which to clear the lane. Before long, another tank had dropped out, stuck fast in the thick mud. The two remaining tanks, however, thrashed their way noisily forward with their giant flails revolving at a frantic pace to begin the task of beating the Red Lane through the enemy minefield. The path was not as wide as it should have been, but the battle had at least begun on time.

The noise stirred up the Germans a short distance away and small arms fire began to zip though the darkness. Before long, mortar and shell fire started coming over. Quite desultory at first, falling randomly all along the line, it gradually became more frequent and accurate, as it attempted to home in on all the noise and activity.

At about the same time, the 1st Battalion of the 334th Regiment began its final move up to the start line. John Mulligan was watching the flail tanks of 'Drew Force' as they beat a clear path through the minefield in front of the orchard. His section was digging slit trenches prior to jumping off into the attack. 'My foxhole buddy, well tanked up from the British rum, was firing his M1 carbine over my head while I was digging our hole, further scaring a bunch of scared kids.'

Lieutenant Melville was in command of Number 4 Troop, from 'B' Squadron of the 1st Lothians and Border Yeomanry. His troop of flail tanks were ordered to clear the Blue Lane through the minefield prior to the attack. At 0600 hours, Melville brought his four tanks through the orchard. He was later to recall:

We followed a line of white tape that had been laid previously by the engineers. Ahead of us were the Sherwood Rangers who led the way in case there were any odd overhanging branches which might damage our jibs. As their tanks emerged from the orchard, they swung left and began to open fire on a suspected enemy position in a house along the main road. They also gave us some covering fire, protecting our left flank. I ran my tank into the open and the remainder of the troop followed. The three flail tanks quickly flailed a path right up to the ditch in front of the railway embankment. It was very dark. Although the searchlights were of some help, I could not see anything at all while closed down inside my tank. I therefore decided to remain head and shoulders out of the cupola to try to see where we were going, occasionally mopping a large daub of mud from my eyes. Luckily, I was able to spot the anti-tank ditch near the railway track in good time. I halted my tank, flailed up and reversed out to one side.

Blue Lane was open for business. Number 4 Troop had finished its main task and now took to the sidelines to give support to the attack that was about to commence.

Close behind the flails came the American engineers, sweeping the route and marking the safe path with white tape. The Sherwood Rangers Yeomanry were now able to move into the gap, ready for the attack.

At five minutes to seven o'clock, the Allied barrage opened up on the German positions. The combined strength of XXX Corps' artillery, supported by all available American guns, pounded the area in front of Briell. The scene was now set: the 'Railsplitters' could enter the war.

At 0700 hours, 'B' Squadron of the Sherwood Rangers, together with its protecting screen of American infantry, passed down the Red Lane towards the railway line. It was still dark and the murky weather made it hard for the drivers to see clearly. The tanks found great difficulty in finding the swept lane owing to the poor type of tape employed in marking the route. There was also another problem; the inaccuracy of the maps given to the flail tank commanders resulted in Red Lane ending up at a point on the railway line which proved to be a tank obstacle. The lane was forced to make a right turn and head parallel to the railway, so as to cross over it about fifty yards to the right of where the gap should have been.

The ground was a sea of mud. The flails had cleared a path through the minefield, but they had also reduced the wet surface to the consistency of soup. The Sherwood Rangers were not going anywhere. Blue Lane soon became impassable to tanks as the M4 Shermans thrashed about up to their bellies in sludge. Red Lane fared little better; some progress was made, but it was soon clear that the ground could not support tanks. The armoured thrust through the German defences was reduced to an infantry assault. Undaunted, the doughboys pushed on through the gaps. In one of the leading groups of infantry was Frank Pinto:

> It was still dark at about 7am when our company, Company A, moved into the orchard at Briell. We advanced in a column of companies: Company A led the first battalion, the first battalion led the 334th Regiment and the 334th Regiment led the whole of the 84th Division. I was the platoon leader of the second platoon and I followed the first platoon over the line of departure which was at the edge of the orchard. I remember being anxious to move out of the orchard because of the shell bursts in the trees from the enemy artillery, but as we emerged from the orchard it was like jumping out of the frying pan and into the fire.

The artillery barrage had stirred up the enemy. He knew that an attack was in progress and retaliated accordingly. Heavy shell and mortar fire now started to scream over and crash amongst the orchards around Briell. Those of the infantry who were in slit trenches had some shelter, but Companies A and E were caught moving up through the trees towards the minefield. Red hot splinters of steel tore through the men and casualties started to mount. Frantic cries of 'medic' went up all around. Just a few moments of combat, and all those years of training counted for nothing to the broken bodies lying in the mud.

Company A led the 1st Battalion's attack on Prummern. It broke through the minefield along Red Lane and soon reached the railway line. Once away from the orchards, it left behind the worst of the shelling. Along the railway embankment, the GIs found a network of German trenches. For the first time, the 'Railsplitters' came face to face with live German soldiers. Fortunately, the enemy were not of high calibre and were easily swamped by the weight of American numbers, although some hand-to-hand fighting did take place.

Company A now formed up along the embankment and looked out towards the battalion's next immediate objective: nine pillboxes clustered together in two groups, protecting the southern approaches to Prummern. The first group consisted of six bunkers set astride the railway line and the Geilenkirchen-Immendorf road, about one thousand yards away. The second group were six hundred yards further north in the direction of Prummern.

The commander of the 1st Battalion, Lieutenant-Colonel Lloyd H. Gomes, had designated these two groups of pillboxes 'X' and 'Y' respectively. During the planning stages of the attack, Gomes had figured out just how he intended to capture them:

> The plan was to have Company A go through the gap and strike hard for 'X', infiltrating through the fortifications and smothering the pillboxes by fire. To assist Company A, we had four tanks, four tank destroyers and one heavy machine gun platoon, together with all the fire support of the mortar platoon and artillery on call. Company B was to jump off after Company A, initially prepared to reinforce Company A's fire and then move on to its objective, 'Y'. Company B was to have one platoon of tanks and one platoon of heavy machine guns with artillery on call.

Unfortunately, there were no tanks available to Company A as it paused in the relative safety of the newly captured German trenches and contemplated the attack. All the armour had stalled in the mud near the start line. Ahead was a thousand yards of open ground with the six pillboxes overlooking every move. Machine gun fire raked the embankment and surrounding fields. Not surprisingly, Company A went to ground for a while waiting for help to arrive. It did not take long, for close on its heels came the 1st Platoon of Company B. But they, also, found the problem a little too difficult to handle. The rest of the company were stuck back in the minefield.

Over to the left, leading the 2nd Battalion on its separate attack towards the high ground west of Prummern, was Company E. On the move up to the start line, the men knew that they were getting closer and closer to the real thing as the noise got louder and the searchlights brighter. Private George Green thought that just about all of his company were suffering from nervous diarrhoea by this time:

> As we approached the front I managed to acquire from somewhere a copy of *Studs Lonigan*, which I was able to read intermittently whenever I had the chance. Unfortunately, I had to tear out pages from time to time for a rather utilitarian purpose. This necessitated my having to attempt to co-ordinate my bodily needs with my intellectual pursuits. Our officers tried to buoy up our morale by reciting actual statistics on how relatively few soldiers were ever wounded in battle and that even fewer of those that were injured ultimately perished.

At 0700 hours, Company E managed to pick its way through the melee of tanks around the minefield and set off along Blue Lane towards the high ground on the Geilenkirchen-Immendorf road around the hamlet of Loherhof. It took an hour to cover the nine hundred yards to this intermediate objective, and the company was shelled all the way. When it finally arrived on the hill, it found a network of trenches and had to fight for the possession of each one. Once again, the troops defending them did not put up too much of a struggle. By 0910 hours the hill was taken. Casualties had been light.

Following behind Company E was Company F. That too had had a relatively easy passage through the minefield. However, the next company, G, was not so fortunate. The moment that it reached the gap in the minefield, the enemy shelling suddenly stepped up in ferocity. Company C from the 1st Battalion had reported inaccurate 88mm fire falling two hundred yards to the right of its gap, but the enemy fire closed in over both gaps before Companies C and G could push their way through. A heavy artillery bombardment from way back in the German rear had now joined in the battle. There was no longer any doubt that a full-scale American attack was underway and interdictory fire was put down on the start line. The whole area erupted in a mass of flame and dirt.

Both companies started a slow infiltration through the gaps, creeping and crawling their way forward. Once on the far side of the minefield the chaos remained. They were unable to reorganise completely until a full two hours later. The four leading companies of the regiment were out in enemy territory on their own.

A short distance away, Lieutenant Melville was parked up in his flail tank watching the action:

Just after dawn broke, the enemy began to send over a thick barrage of large calibre shells. The fire was fairly accurate and all of my troop of tanks were scarred by pieces of shrapnel. My own periscope was splintered by a near miss. Several American soldiers were lying on the ground around our positions, either dead or badly wounded, but we could do nothing to help them.

Although the two lanes through the minefield were still under constant shelling, the tanks of the Sherwood Rangers had gradually begun to extricate themselves from the mire. Blue Lane was however, beyond redemption – the ground there was impassable. In consequence, all the tanks of 'B' Squadron were ordered to move over to the Red Lane exit. By 0900 hours, a few Shermans from each squadron had made it out into open country and raced off to join up with the infantry. Others followed throughout the remainder of the morning.

Lieutenant-Colonel Gomes moved forward to join his leading two companies on the railway embankment. He found them pinned down by enemy machine gun fire. He desperately needed to get the momentum going again:

I moved forward to contact Captain Woodrow Fox, commanding Company A, and learned what was holding them up. When I saw Captain Fox I realised that he would not be able to push his company through and get to the objective as rapidly as desired. I was convinced that bold, aggressive action at this time would save many lives, because we had to close with the fortifications before they could open up on us from long range. Most of Company A had taken positions along the railroad track and would not budge.

The battalion commander went down the platoons, one by one, urging their leaders to get the troops moving forward again. The platoon leaders were all second lieutenants, but Gomes knew they were excellent officers. He started one platoon moving, then another. The situation was given added impetus with the arrival of tanks. The two companies gradually put their fears behind them and advanced across open sugar beet fields.

John Mulligan remembers being along the railway line during this advance.

Several of us were lying in a shell hole taking cover from the sniper and artillery fire not knowing what to do next. When I looked up, I saw the Battalion Commander, Lieutenant-Colonel Lloyd Gomes, standing at the rim of the crater. He was yelling at us to move forward, which we did immediately. I have a lot of respect for that man; he led his troops from the front.

While the battalion's heavy machine guns and Sherwood Rangers peppered the pillboxes with fire, the two infantry companies set off across the sugar beet fields to capture them. Ed Epstein was with one of the heavy machine guns during the attack. His squad was to maintain a continuous barrage of fire onto the pillbox slits to ensure that the German defenders closed them and kept their heads down. As long as they did this, the men inside were virtually blind.

Company A swept across the exposed middle ground with little opposition. In front of the first pillbox was a warren of interwoven dugouts leading back to the concrete bunker. The trenches were empty. The defenders had fled inside. For a while there was stalemate. The pillboxes were too strong to reduce by shellfire and too powerful to be bypassed and left intact in the rear. 'After a long pause for someone to come up with a good idea,' recalls Frank Pinto, 'someone crawled on top of the pillbox and dropped a smoke grenade down the ventilator pipe. About forty Germans surrendered.'

From then on the going was easier; the tanks and machine guns kept the pillboxes closed up, while the infantry overran them. Then smoke grenades were dropped down the ventilator shaft and the trapped enemy soldiers inside surrendered en masse. Within an hour, the six pillboxes designated 'X' by Colonel Gomes were captured and disarmed.

Company B had similar success with the 'Y' group of three pillboxes to the north. It still had only one platoon up on the railway embankment. Its others were in a disorganised state, struggling through the shellfire back in the minefield. Nonetheless, Gomes ordered the 1st Platoon to begin the attack on the three pillboxes. He was determined that the momentum was not going to be allowed to falter. By this time, two Shermans from 'A' Squadron of the Sherwood Rangers had joined up with the 1st Platoon just as it was about to launch the attack. Tanks and infantry moved out together. About three hundred yards short of the pillboxes they stopped and the tanks opened fire, concentrating on the small weapons slits at the front of the bunkers. Then the infantry went on alone, closing on the pillboxes, firing from the hip. Just in front of the objective was a complex network of trenches, surrounding the three pillboxes and linking them back to the village of Prummern. The earthworks should have enabled the enemy to bring up reinforcements without them being exposed to Allied observation, but events had unfurled too quickly for them to make use of them. The American troops were in the trenches before the German soldiers could react. Some of the defenders ran back to the pillboxes, while others tried to make it back to the village. The GIs were, however, much too close and any attempts at withdrawal were suicidal.

It took only forty-five minutes for the 1st Platoon to reduce the three pillboxes. None of the defenders locked up inside attempted to fire. The Americans had caught them blind. In theory, the pillboxes were designed to give one another mutual support when under attack. The men inside should have provided each adjacent emplacement with covering fire to beat off any attempts by assaulting troops to get too close but, once they had closed up the slits, they had reduced the bunkers to nothing more than concrete coffins. The only way out was surrender, or death. The troops from the 183rd Volks Grenadier Division chose surrender.

The pillboxes captured, the battalion's main objective was now in sight. The village of Prummern lay just five hundred yards away across the fields, but it would take more than just the 1st Platoon of Company B to capture it. The remainder of the company had still not made it up to the pillboxes, so the order was given to dig in and await reinforcements.

Lieutenant-Colonel Gomes was pleased with events so far. The nine pillboxes guarding the approaches to Prummern had been captured with fewer casualties than had been expected. It was time for the assault on Prummern itself. He put Company A into reserve and ordered Companies B and C to prepare to attack the village just as soon as they had reorganised themselves into position.

The morning was also going quite well for the 2nd Battalion. Company F had moved over the first hill around the hamlet of Loherhof, captured earlier by Company E, and then set out for the next piece of high ground. Tanks from 'B' Squadron of the Sherwood Rangers had made it forward, in spite of the intensity of the enemy shelling and the bad state of the ground, to be up with the leading platoons as they moved out across the open hillside. This was just as well, for the next spur contained four well sited pillboxes.

Three of the pillboxes were sited around a 'Y' shaped road junction, with a fourth located on slightly lower ground to the west. The Sherman tanks overtook the soldiers on foot and made it to the pillboxes first. Here they kept the defenders occupied by direct fire from their 75mm guns and co-axially mounted machine guns. The fire was aimed at the apertures through which the enemy were retaliating. Major Peter Selerie was in command of the squadron:

Shortly after we opened up on the pillboxes, the leading elements of the infantry arrived. They had advanced bravely, but had unfortunately suffered a number of casualties. Those who survived very soon started to descend and penetrate the various galleries and tunnels of these formidable fortifications. German prisoners with their hands up began to emerge like rabbits from a warren. There was great feeling of satisfaction amongst us. After the hard slog across France, Belgium and Holland, we were finally on the Siegfried Line.

Selerie dismounted from his tank and joined the 2nd Battalion's commander, Lieutenant-Colonel James Drum in one of the captured posts where he had established battalion headquarters. Drum was concerned that his half-tracks with their anti-tank guns had bogged down near the start line. There were no guns up with the leading troops. Selerie immediately ordered one of his Shermans to go back down the hill to tow up the cannons. A short while later, at 1035 hours, Lieutenant-Colonel Drum was injured and had to be evacuated. Command passed to Major Eleazer, the battalion's Executive Officer.

Situation at 1117 hours, Saturday, 18 November
The 334th Regiment had made a good start in this its first action. The 1st Battalion had captured the strongpoints commanding the southern approaches to its main objective, the village of Prummern. The 2nd Battalion had covered two thirds of the distance to its final objective, Hill 101 due west of Prummern. Casualties up to that point had been remarkably light. The outer crust of the Siegfried Line had been pierced successfully. It was now time to tackle the core of Hitler's Westwall.

Chapter Six

Prummern

At 1118 hours, Colonel John Roosma, Commander of the 334th Regiment, was handed a message that came as something of a shock to him. British XXX Corps had discovered that an enemy force of four thousand five hundred men were at that moment en route for Geilenkirchen. Aerial reconnaissance had spotted a column of tanks and vehicles three and a half miles long heading south from Heinsberg. Intelligence suggested that these were more troops from the 15th Panzer Grenadier Division, which had units already operating in the area.

Roosma had been half expecting a counter attack to come at him from Prummern, where the 9th Panzer Division was known to have reserves bolstering up the German front line. The 9th Panzers had already been in action that day against the US 2nd Armored Division on Roosma's right. He also knew that enemy troops in Geilenkirchen would always be a danger to his left flank, should they launch an attack from that direction. However, the German troop movements of the size spotted by the British were something that had not been foreseen. If the 15th Panzer Grenadiers reinforced Geilenkirchen within the next few hours, not only would his regiment be at risk, but the whole division also.

Roosma acted quickly. First, he ordered the 1st Battalion to hold its attack on Prummern. Next, he requested time fire from the artillery to be placed along the southern edge of the village every ten minutes, to discourage any enemy counter attack. He then ordered his reserve battalion, the 3rd Battalion, up to the area of high ground behind the 2nd Battalion around the hamlet of Loherhof, to protect his left flank. If the enemy came out of Geilenkirchen at his regiment, then he would be ready. Once all these moves were in place, the attack on Prummern could go ahead.

Roosma was not the only commander concerned with the news of the enemy reinforcements. Both Horrocks and Bolling had also noticed the danger and were taking steps to counter it. Normally, an American infantry division is composed of three regiments. During an attack, one of these is kept in reserve. However, Bolling's 84th Division had only two regiments under command because its third, the 335th, was on loan to the 30th Infantry Division. To replace this regiment, the 405th Regiment had been assigned to the division from the US 102nd Infantry Division, but the 405th were still in the line, holding the area to the east of Geilenkirchen that the 'Railsplitters' were attacking through.

Brigadier-General Bolling now called upon his erstwhile Corps Commander, Major-General Gillem, for help. Gillem was in command of the US XIII Corps, on the right of the British XXX Corps. He immediately pledged his reserve, the 407th Regiment, to Bolling for use in counter attack should the 'Railsplitters' come under pressure. In addition, the 405th Regiment was ordered to assemble itself ready to counter attack to the north–west should this become necessary. With the front thus stabilised, Operation Clipper could continue as planned.

By 1150 hours, Companies B and C of the 1st Battalion had made it up past the captured pillboxes and were ready to carry on the attack on Prummern. Artillery fire, together with some direct fire from the tanks of the Sherwood Rangers, was concentrated along the eastern edge of the village. Ten minutes later the attack went in, Company C on the left, Company B on the right.

News that the attack on Prummern had begun was passed over to the British 43rd Division. Major-General Thomas had been waiting anxiously for this message. His division was set to begin its own attack on the western side of Geilenkirchen at 1215 hours, as part of the planned encirclement of the town. Now that the 334th Regiment had started its final attack, the way was clear for the British to begin with theirs.

As the 'Railsplitters' swept across the open ground towards Prummern, they were met by machine gun and sniper fire from the trenches and foxholes on the outskirts of the village. The advance continued across the flat terrain, bare of any concealment. Some platoons were lucky enough to escape the worst of the fire. Others caught the full force: 'I went from first gunner to section leader that day, as the squad leader and section leader were both hit', recalled Ed Epstein, a member of a less fortunate platoon. 'I remember putting sulpha powder on the section leader's wound and bandaging it before he went back for medical treatment. I thought he had a flesh wound on the side of his chest, but it turned out that the injury involved a broken rib that punctured his lung. He died later that day.'

The area in front of Prummern was heavily mined. 'A' Squadron of the Sherwood Rangers lost a number of tanks during the attack. One of them belonged to the Squadron Commander, Major John Semken, whose Sherman passed over a cluster of four mines, setting them all off simultaneously. Fortunately, none of the crew were hurt. Semken dismounted and moved to take over another tank. This, too, hit a mine and the major moved to yet another tank. Unbelievably, that tank was also blown up by a mine. Following this, word went back down the line that the major was 'missing'. Reverend Leslie Skinner, the chaplain to the Sherwood Rangers, was in the area at the time:

> I found Major Semken sitting in a burnt out pillbox, reading poetry if I remember right. He was somewhat surprised to learn that no one knew where he was. Truth to tell he was somewhat shaken. We chatted for a time and then walked out together, by which time he had more or less recovered his customary blase chatter.

Enemy resistance to the attack continued, but was mostly from light weapons. The infantry pushed on defiantly, stopping only to clear out trenches and foxholes along the route. On the outskirts of the buildings, more defences and trench networks were found and cleared of enemy troops. At around 1300 hours, the two companies at last entered Prummern. At this point, some fifty Germans, hands clasped above their heads, were awaiting removal to the rear.

The tricky job of clearing the buildings now took place. A hand grenade into each house and cellar helped to convince those of the enemy still remaining to quit. Prisoners tumbled out of every conceivable hiding place. Companies B and C made good progress and by 1410 were through the village and digging in on the outskirts of the far side. The 1st Battalion was now in Prummern, but it was not the complete master of the village. There was still a great deal of mopping up to be done. Lieutenant-Colonel Gomes, 1st Battalion's commander explained:

> We brought Company A in to mop up the town, isolated pockets of resistance still existed in the north-eastern section of Prummern at 1530 hours; elements of Companies B and C were ordered to clear this sector.
>
> Recognising the possibility of counter attacks, I ordered Company B disposed in the orchard on the western edge of the town, Company C in the orchard to the north and Company A to the southwest. It took quite some time to organise positions that would hold against attack.

Up with these leading companies was Private John Mulligan. It had been an eventful day for him. Mulligan set out that morning as the fourth ammunition bearer in a mortar squad. It did not take him long to learn that ammunition bags that fit over the head cause the body to stick up when you hit the ground. He was quick to appreciate that if you twist the bags so that they laid on each shoulder, a lower silhouette was produced when lying in the dirt after the shelling started.

I don't remember the number of casualties on that first day, but I do know that I went from 4th ammunition bearer to 1st gunner before the day was out, due to the rest of the squad being hit. Since I had only fired two mortar rounds in my life, and both of them while training in England, I wasn't too well equipped to handle the job.

Meanwhile, further to the west of the 1st Battalion, the 2nd Battalion was keeping abreast of the attack on Prummern. By 1510 hours, it too had reached its main objective, Hill 101, 1,500 yards due west of the village. The going had been hard, both for the men and for the tanks. 'B' Squadron of the Sherwood Rangers had one Sherman knocked out by mines and several others bogged down in the thick mud. The surface of the ground seemed to have the consistency of sticky clay. Efforts by an armoured recovery team to extract the mined tank failed to move it an inch.

With the offensive part of the operation concluded and the infantry safely digging in on their final position, it was time for the tanks to withdraw. Major Selerie told the battalion commander that his squadron would draw back about a mile to rendezvous with the rear echelon trucks, to replenish with fuel, ammunition and rations:

> The battle had been so intense that we had very little ammunition left in spite of our entirely irregular custom of erecting a pyramid of 75mm shells under the gun. In addition, I said that we would remain in leaguer so that the tank crews could snatch a few hours sleep. I promised to be back with the battalion before first light.

It was a depressing evening with drizzling rain. The Sherman tanks churned their way through the mud and eventually found the lane that led back to their rendezvous. Suddenly from the side of the road, there appeared a slightly lame enemy infantryman shouting 'Kamerad'. Selerie told his driver to stop. The sorry-looking German soldier turned his face up to the major and exclaimed in rather bad English, 'War no good.' Selerie motioned the man to climb up on the front of the tank and ordered his driver to continue on down the road. The German was taken back for interrogation.

The German troops in and around Prummern that day were, as predicted, mainly from the 183rd Volks Grenadier Division, commanded by Generalleutnant Wolfgang Lange. Although his troops were manning the defences, Lange had been ordered to relinquish control of the area to the two other German units operating in the vicinity, the 15th Panzer Grenadier Division and the 9th Panzer Division. As General Lange explained after the war, he was not happy with the decision:

The 183rd Volks Grenadier gave up control of this sector to those two divisions, but was not authorised to remove its troops. Even those whose combat value had sunk to a minimum during the preceding fighting were required to remain. Once again, the disadvantage of mixing units or postponing their reorganisation was evident. Any unit is at its worst when fighting as part of another unit; a unit tends to abuse another unit subordinate to it.

The morale of Lange's troops had plummeted. They had been fighting in a purely defensive role around Geilenkirchen since mid-September. They had witnessed the front line being steadily pushed further and further back until they were finally lodged in the thick fortifications of the Westwall. After each American attack, they had been methodically ordered to launch a futile counter attack with their depleted forces to recapture the lost ground. To many, it seemed that they were being now being asked to make a last stand on the last defensive line at the frontier with the West. Failure here would let the invading Allied armies through into the heartland of Germany. The war was beginning to seem irretrievably lost.

Colonel Roosma had good reason to feel pleased with the performance of the 334th Regiment in this its first day of combat. By mid-afternoon, it had taken all the objectives allocated to the regiment. Although Prummern was still being cleared of the enemy, control of the village was firmly in the hands of the 1st Battalion. Casualties amongst the 'Railsplitters' had been acceptable. The Regiment had lost 190 men killed or wounded, while the enemy suffered 450 casualties and had 330 men taken prisoner.

The men of the 334th had acquired their experience of life at the sharp end through this baptism of fire. Each had now earned themselves the coveted right to wear the infantryman's combat badge, denoting that the holder had seen action.

In achieving his targets with several hours of daylight left, Roosma had landed his regiment with another job. What had originally been his final objectives for the day, now merely became intermediate ones. The Divisional Commander had decided to keep up the momentum and take advantage of the regiment's successes. Bolling ordered Roosma to push the 334th on a little further before nightfall. The 1st Battalion was now to take Hill 92.5 (codenamed 'Mahogany Hill') to the north east of Prummern, while the 2nd Battalion was to place a company on the next area of high ground to the north east of Hill 101 and gain a position overlooking the village of Suggerath.

General Bolling had been assisted in his decision by an order that afternoon from Horrocks, the British Corps Commander, which stated that the 84th Division should combine the third and fourth phases of the battle the next day. This meant that the 'Railsplitters' were now required to take Geilenkirchen and

Suggerath as planned with the 333rd Regiment, but also to launch the 334th Regiment against the three villages of Mullendorf, Beeck and Wurm to the north. Both of these major actions would be greatly assisted by the capture of the two new areas of high ground that the 1st and 2nd Battalions were now ordered to advance on.

Late in the afternoon, Colonel Roosma passed on the instructions to his battalion commanders in the field. Lieutenant-Colonel Gomes was with his men in Prummern:

> At about 1630 a Company C platoon leader informed my headquarters that an enemy tank on the northern edge of the village was firing at his positions.
>
> We reported this to the British tank commander supporting us, but he said he could not do anything about it due to the fact that the enemy tank was on dominating terrain. We had no other weapons with us to combat it, so we set up 57mm anti-tank guns and mortars on the road to prevent the tank entering the town.
>
> At about the same time, I received an order from Colonel Roosma, which stated that I would have to move one company forward and take the high ground to the northwest, coded 'Mahogany Hill'. I pointed out the danger of enemy infiltration into the town, but he insisted.

As the damp wet day faded into twilight, British searchlights came forward to produce a reflected glow over the area of Prummern. The gathering darkness now gave some much needed cover to small parties of the enemy who began slipping back into the village. Even as the new plans for the continued advance were being put into effect, resistance in the village continued to increase. The ruined buildings provided perfect concealment for the enemy snipers who were making the streets untenable with their harassing fire. Hostile artillery added to the battalion's discomfort. The initial drive and enthusiasm it had felt earlier in the day, increased by its early successes, was now beginning to wane. The 'Railsplitters' were cold, muddy, hungry, tired and under increasingly vicious counter fire.

From his command post in a bombed-out cellar, Colonel Gomes gave instructions for a patrol from Company B to effect a reconnaissance and find a route up to Mahogany Hill for the rest of the company. It was dark by the time the patrol finally set out. The move was the start of an attack that was to last a further four days. Mahogany Hill, just a few hundred yards north east of the village held by the battalion, did not fall to the 'Railsplitters' until 22 November.

Meanwhile, the 2nd Battalion continued with its advance across the high ground towards the new objective above Suggerath. Company F was ordered forward to capture the next spur. It was soon halted by intense artillery and mortar fire. There was now no question that the enemy had recognised the 84th Division's advance as a major attack and he was intent on resisting every move. It could only be a matter of time before he put in his own counter attack against the Americans.

Situation at 1700 hours, Saturday, 18 November
The British attack had gone in at 1215 hours that morning. Reports reaching the 84th Division from XXX Corps HQ about the British assault were encouraging. The American 334th Regiment had completed a good day's work. It had taken its main objectives and was even now pushing on to take new ground. The German resistance had been less determined than first envisaged. There was every hope that next day would bring even better results as further pressure was put on the German 183rd Volks Grenadier Division by the attack on Geilenkirchen by the 333rd Regiment.

Chapter Seven

The British Attack

At about the same time that the American 334th Regiment started the offensive against Prummern, the British 214 Brigade began its move from Brunssum in Holland to the assembly area, in preparation for its assault to the west of Geilenkirchen shortly after noon. At 0830 hours, the brigade crossed the border into Germany. It was an historic occasion, for, although 129 Brigade had been holding a defensive line inside Germany for the last few days, 214 Brigade had taken over the mantle of the attacker. Now, at last, after five long years of bitter struggle against the Nazis in other lands, the British had finally brought the war home to German soil.

At Niederbusch, the troops de-bussed on the road to Gilrath and dug themselves into the sandy soil. Not a single shell or mortar disturbed the assembly. None of the division's previous battles had ever opened in such a peaceful setting. The historian of the 1st Worcestershires describes the scene:

> To our surprise, we found a hot meal waiting for us. Fortified with food, tea and a rum issue, and happily reinforced with fatalism and a characteristic lack of imagination, we waited for the order to move up to the forming-up point, all the while listening to the steadily increasing artillery build-up.

214 Brigade's objective was the occupation of the string of villages around the north-western side of Geilenkirchen, the most important of which was Bauchem, a suburb of the town. This village had been assigned to the 5th Dorsets, on loan to the brigade from 130 Brigade. The assault on Bauchem was to be the last action of what was to be a four battalion attack. First, the 7th Somerset Light Infantry would advance due east and secure the village of Niederheide. Next, the 1st Worcestershires would veer slightly to the north and capture the woods to the left of Niederheide, the village of Rischden and, finally, Tripsrath. After that, came the 5th Duke of Cornwall's Light Infantry, who intended to move up through the Somersets, carry on eastwards to take Hocheid and then finally swing south to seize the high ground overlooking the

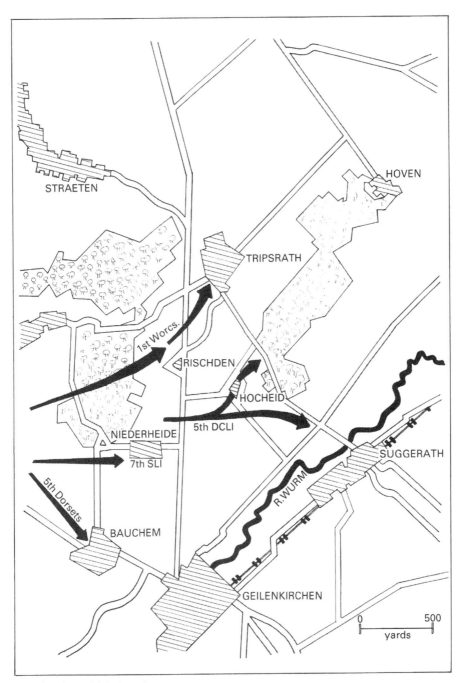

Map 4: The British Attack.

main road into Geilenkirchen from the north. The 5th Dorsets would then take Bauchem.

The 7th Somersets were to lead off the attack. The battalion formed up in a huge sand quarry near the Gilrath brickworks, awaiting the start of the artillery barrage. At 1200 hours, news arrived at Divisional HQ that on the American side of the River Wurm, the final attack by the 334th Regiment had gone in. All was set for the British action to begin. The enemy were completely oblivious of the pending British assault and remained quiet.

At 1217 hours, the guns opened up. For the next twelve minutes over two hundred and fifty pieces of artillery pulverised Bauchem. The village disappeared in a cloud of dust, flame and smoke. At 1230 hours, the guns lifted their concentration and diverted their attention to the site of the Somersets' impending attack. However, the pounding of Bauchem did not let up. The barrage was taken up by an assortment of weapons: anti-tank guns, anti-aircraft cannons, heavy mortars and tanks, all hammered the village. It was a deluge that was to continue unabated until the Dorsets put in their attack over three hours later. Brigadier Essame, Commander of 214 Brigade, later commented that it was doubtful whether any locality in the whole campaign received a more intense bombardment.

With its right flank and the enemy in Bauchem now safely taken care of, the 7th Somersets could launch its assault. At 1230 hours, the infantry, supported by a squadron of tanks from the 4th/7th Royal Dragoon Guards, moved across the start line and out into the open field.

The soft going immediately began to take its toll of any vehicle trying to cross the open ground between Gilrath and Niederheide. Tank after tank sank into the mire. Carriers and anti-tank guns floundered in the sprocket-deep liquid mud. The chaos quickly stretched back to the start line and beyond.

Thirty minutes after the 7th Somersets had gone over to the attack, the 1st Worcestershires began the move to its start line. The battalion marched down the road to Gilrath in high spirits. Along the verge were representatives of the Press, filming the attack for cinema audiences at home. Although the battalion was by now rather blase about being at the point of the action, once again making history, the Worcestershires were, nonetheless, still thrilled to think they would be in the News.

As the infantrymen wound their way through the desolate remains of Gilrath, each step bringing them closer to the sounds of battle, they became a little more subdued. The dry mouth and familiar clenched feeling gripping the stomach returned, as each man quietly fought his own lonely battle against the all-pervasive fear of the unknown. Some sought escape in exaggerated humour. The joker raised an occasional polite laugh from his sober mates around him to help to relieve the tension. The Commanding Officer, Lieutenant-Colonel R.

Osborne Smith, with a rifle nonchalantly slung over his shoulder, moved quietly among the troops seemingly unconcerned, chatting to his men lying on the ground. Officers stared intently at their watches, following the sweep of the second hand as it marked off the remaining few minutes. It was almost time to go.

At 1400 hours, Osborne Smith gave the order to start. The two leading companies, B and C, got to their feet and set off into the noise and smoke.

The first objective was a wood to the north of Niederheide. Little opposition was met while crossing the open ground. The first death was caused by a friendly artillery shell falling short. In front of the wood C Company encountered a minefield. It caused little serious delay, for the recent wet weather had removed most of the soil leaving the mines poking through the mud in full view. The leading infantry cautiously picked their way through the deadly maze, leaving the engineers following behind to deal with the hazard. Next there was a labyrinth of barbed wire to negotiate. But this, too, failed to check the Worcestershires. They were veterans of many actions and quickly found the well worn track through the tangle of wire made by the daily comings and goings of enemy soldiers. The company pressed on into the woods and there met the first real opposition.

Enemy infantry were in the woods and so were their mines, schu mines. These deadly anti-personnel weapons caused tragic injuries. When trodden on, the mine would fire a charge six feet into the air which then exploded and showered the area with shrapnel. There was little defence against this unpleasant weapon. Once encountered, men would often become paralysed with fear. Only the most highly trained infantry would press on with an attack in such a minefield. For a short while momentum was lost. Then, slowly, cautiously, order was regained. A way was found through the area. Moving in a single column to minimise the risk of setting off a mine, the advance continued. Nonetheless, it was hazardous. A platoon sergeant had his foot blown off when he stepped on a mine. Once clear of the minefield, the Worcestershires ran up against the next obstacle: the enemy.

'He in fact behaved in a most extraordinary manner,' relates the battalion's historian. 'He was sincerely pleased to see British troops upon whom he pressed his watch and other trinkets in demonstration of his gratitude.' The German troops were pale and shaken from the artillery barrage and were happy to give up without a fight, content to be passed back to the rear of the British lines into the prisoner-of-war cages. All the prisoners were from the 183rd Volks Grenadier Division.

Further over to the left, B Company had sidestepped the thick woods and were making straight for Rischden, another 1,000 yards forward. Lieutenant Rex Fellows was crossing the open ground with his platoon:

Ahead of us I could see a mixture of fire coming down. Some of it was DF fire from the Germans and some from our own artillery. I remember thinking to myself, 'I wonder if we are going to get safely by, or get caught in the middle of it.' We managed to get into an area of thin woods and scrubland without problems and then found that some of the shelling was falling behind us out in the open. It looked as though the timing of the creeping barrage was not quite right.

The company took the village with little opposition in evidence. Rex Fellows had moved his platoon across the thick undergrowth.

There were teller mines lying about exposed, just as though they had been chucked on the ground. There did not seem to be any attempt to conceal them. My platoon passed through without any casualties. We carried on towards the village using our usual technique of putting a lot of lead forward to keep the other buggers' heads down. When we got to Rischden it was empty. I don't believe there was ever anybody there, unless they had scarpered as we came in.

Fellows and his platoon now approached their final objective, a pillbox covering the road junction to the north east of the village. At least, the map said that there was a pillbox there, but Fellows could find nothing. So, having reached his objective in the approved manner, he told his men to dig in as quickly as possible because the Germans were sure to retaliate at the loss of the village. He chose positions in the open just north of the village and to the left of the main road.

At this point, C Company was immediately ordered to join up with B Company and establish a firm base in Rischden ready for the next phase of the action. This first stage of the attack had gone well. Although no tanks had been able to get through the mud to join the battalion, these two companies had, nonetheless, taken the intermediate objectives, and the Worcestershires were now preparing for the final assault on Tripsrath by A and D Companies. Then things began to go wrong.

Between Rischden and C Company was a square copse. The Worcestershires' Carrier Platoon had been ordered to seize this small wood once Rischden had been taken. By this time they had struggled through the mud and chaos at the start line and now moved up the track alongside the small wood to take possession of it. At this moment, the enemy chose to counter the Worcestershires' progress. Two self-propelled guns manoeuvred themselves to the edge of the thick woods to the north of Rischden and opened fire. They had the range to the yard; the Carrier Platoon had no chance. One by one, the small tracked vehicles were blown to pieces. In the space of a few minutes, the platoon was virtually wiped out and thirty-one broken bodies littered the grassy track.

Events now continued to go wrong. A short while later, Rischden was shelled. The Worcestershires' Commanding Officer had just moved into the village with his advance HQ when a salvo of shells fell among them. Colonel Osborne Smith was hit and was immediately evacuated. The second-in-command was back in Holland with the rear echelon. The battalion was leaderless. It could not have happened at a worse time. The first phase of the operation was complete, Rischden was secure, but what of the attack on Tripsrath? The adjutant set out to find the next most senior officer to take charge. He ran around the forward companies searching for Major John Ricketts.

With Niederheide and Rischden now safely in the hands of 214 Brigade, it was time for Brigadier Essame to launch his third battalion, the 5th Duke of Cornwall's Light Infantry, into the battle. Its Commanding Officer, Lieutenant-Colonel George Taylor, had played a great part in the difficult task of getting his battalion up to the start line on time. They too, had been bogged down in the traffic jams around Gilrath, as they moved slowly forward along the only approach road. The route was cluttered with the carriers, anti-tank guns and jeeps of the 7th Somersets and 1st Worcestershires. Determined that his battalion would keep to its tight schedule, Taylor paced up and down the line, shouting orders and encouragement at his men through a megaphone. He bullied and blustered them forward, by-passing the worst of the hold ups.

The Cornwalls' forming up point for its attack was a square copse, just back from a lane leading from Niederheide to Rischden. The battalion's objectives for the attack were, first, the village of Hocheid, then, the woods immediately behind, and finally and most importantly of all, to swing right and cut the main road into Geilenkirchen from the rear.

At a few minutes to three o'clock, the leading troops of D Company began to move out from cover and made their way to the start line. Some tanks from the 4th/7th Royal Dragoon Guards had managed to make their way up to the Cornwalls and were now lined up ready to support the attack.

In the middle of the road that was the start line, D Company's immaculate Commander, Major Michael Lonsdale, wearing his best battle-dress and carrying a cane, moved quietly among the leading platoon, giving his men a final briefing. He pointed out the line of German trenches just short of the village that was their first objective. The village of Hocheid was a short distance beyond, behind a wire fence.

At 1500 hours, the familiar swish and roar of incoming shells passing low overhead heralded the start of the artillery barrage, right on time. Seconds later, a few hundred yards to the front, flashes of brilliant red and yellow marked the shells' arrival on target. The area ahead of the Cornwalls was being softened up by the combined firepower of two hundred and fifty guns from corps and divisional artillery.

Major Lonsdale had asked the gunners for a clear signal when they had come to the end of their barrage:

> Gunners and supporting arms always think that every infantryman has got a watch, and that he has got time to look at the watch, but that is not so. I had arranged for the battery commander to give me a signal when he was lifting the fire. He asked me what I would like. I said, 'Give me blue and red smoke and I'm off!'

After plastering the whole area with high explosive, the barrage began to lift, finally ending with a concentration of red and blue smoke shells on the village and the forward edge of the wood beyond. As soon as D Company had cleared the start line, the Dragoon Guards' Sherman tanks roared through the gap at great speed to support the assault. Within minutes, they had all disappeared into the mist along with the first wave of infantry.

The first two platoons could not count on surprise to outwit the enemy after such a long bombardment, so they were determined to get at him the moment he came out from shelter. The Cornwalls broke cover and charged across the open ground at the outer trenches firing wildly from the hip. Within minutes they were among the dugouts, attacking the defenders with their rifles and bayonets. This first line of defence was carried without loss.

Next came the wire fence. Here the infantry met trouble. A German Spandau away to the left was firing along the line of wire and each man had to run a gauntlet of machine gun bullets to get forward. Several men lay down on the top of the wire to help others over and the leading troops were soon in the village. Within a short time they had disappeared among the houses.

By the time Major Lonsdale had got forward, no one was to be seen. Lonsdale managed to cross the wire to a fanfare of bullets from the enemy machine gun and passed up the main street. He commented:

> I think my soldiers went through the village a little too quickly without searching every house. I thought I saw a German coat in one of the houses as I passed up the road and realised there might be some of the enemy still around. Coming down the street towards me was one of my chaps. He had been wounded, but was fit enough to give me covering fire to get into the house. I got him to lie down with his rifle pointing at the door. I begged him not to shoot me as I went in. I didn't care a damn how many Germans he shot, but wanted him to make sure he missed me. Then I drew my revolver and pushed my way in through the door. I was confronted by a group of the enemy who looked absolutely staggered to see me. I was not sure who was the more frightened, them or me. I grunted at them and waved them outside with my pistol. Nineteen of the brutes filed out of the

house! They all threw down their arms and were escorted back down the line by my one wounded private.

B Company now emerged cautiously from the forming up point in the square copse and made their way to the command post Colonel Taylor had set up on the road. They moved forward hesitantly, in open order. Taylor again made good use of his megaphone to maintain direction and momentum:

> All this activity had stirred the enemy into a savage reaction. Heavy shells whined overhead from the east and crashed into the woods amongst the Worcestershires. Then the range shortened and ugly black bursts began to appear ahead along the road where the line of khaki figures were moving. The shelling was intense and accurate and a line of figures suddenly broke for the open in a bid to side-step this horror of bursting explosive and steel. It turned out to be the headquarters of the 1st Worcestershires. I didn't realise this and used my megaphone, shouting, 'Stop that bloody nonsense!' Their CO was wounded in this shelling.

Meanwhile, Lonsdale had brought up his reserve platoon into Hocheid and now set about taking the woods beyond the village. The major went forward to do a reconnaissance and found all was well. D Company's two forward platoons were ordered to advance and capture the neck of the woods about two hundred yards from the village. The troops moved ahead noisily firing from the hip once again and raking the neighbourhood with Bren gun fire. By 1645 hours, it had been occupied without difficulty and the Cornwalls set about arranging its defence. A strong patrol was sent out to check the forward area and brought back a huge SS sergeant, who was found to have on his person a map of the whole of the enemy's minefields in the surrounding sector.

Thirty minutes after the 5th Duke of Cornwall's Light Infantry had begun its attack on Hocheid, the 5th Dorsets set out on its assault on Bauchem. The village was the key to the whole success of the first phase of the battle. This suburb of Geilenkirchen housed a considerable number of the enemy and threatened the 43rd Division's right flank. To Major-General Thomas, it was vital that Bauchem was completely neutralised as quickly as possible.

To this end, it had been subjected to continuous bombardment for over three hours. Initially, all the guns of the Corps had been concentrated on the village but, as the various attacks by 214 Brigade went in, more and more of the artillery had been switched to give support elsewhere. Nonetheless, a tremendous weight of explosive metal continued to descend on Bauchem from smaller calibre weapons, throughout the afternoon. Then, with five minutes to go before the attack, all available guns returned to bombard the village once more.

Major George Loosley was the Battery Commander of the 220th Field Battery, part of the 112th Field Regiment Royal Artillery. Loosley's battery of 25 pounder field guns had supported the 5th Dorsets in every action. Once again, they were lined up in the rear ready to fire the battalion into the attack. Loosley had had plenty of time to reconnoitre the area. He was dismayed at the ground over which the Dorsets were preparing to advance – 1,500 yards of flat, open country with no cover. He feared for the safety of his own forward observers and decided to minimise any risk to them. He would coordinate the support fire and observe the advance from the high ground on the right flank:

I had consulted with the Commanding Officer of the 5th Dorsets and decided that, as we had excellent communications with his HQ, and seeing that there was a set fire plan for the attack, which would not be varied, my forward artillery observation officer, Captain Gilders, would remain at the start line until the Dorsets reached the outskirts of Bauchem. I was concerned for the safety of Captain Gilders. He was an old friend. I have the impression that the expectation of life for an artillery troop commander was about one month. Gilders had been in the front line for over five months.

Captain Jack Gilders would survive this attack, but it was to be his last.

The traffic chaos in Gilrath continued with little sign of improvement. All transport moving forward was delayed by stranded vehicles. The battalion would have to move off without tank support, for the 13th/18th Kings Royal Hussars became bogged down in the thick mud as they tried to move up to the start line. Nonetheless, morale was high. Preparations for the attack had been thorough; each man in the battalion knew exactly where he had to go and what he had to do.

Although the forming-up point for the attack was fairly obvious, the area did not receive any hostile shelling. The enemy was being kept busy elsewhere trying to cope with 214 Brigade's operations to the north. At precisely 1530 hours, the set piece attack went in.

The approach to the village lay across almost a mile of open country. The sight of the battalion deployed for action was reminiscent of pictures of the Great War, as wave after wave rose up and moved forward. The two forward companies were soon on their first objective, a line of trenches about three hundred yards from the village.

In one of those German trenches was a twenty-one year old sergeant called Peter Brauweiler. He had been posted to the 183rd Volks Grenadier Division a month previously, from NCO Training School. He was a veteran of the Russian campaign, with a great deal of combat experience. Since arriving at the front he had seen little action, for the section of the line around Bauchem was a quiet spot.

Although everyone in his battalion knew that the Americans had attacked on the far side of Geilenkirchen, nobody was expecting the British to do anything. As far as they were concerned, they were merely holding the line. It came as something of a shock when the artillery barrage began just after midday, and the ferocity of the bombardment was worse than anything Brauweiler had ever experienced:

> For over three hours we were subjected to continual artillery fire. All of the buildings around us were reduced to piles of smoking rubble. We just crouched in our trenches and suffered. Then, through the smoke, I saw the British coming at us. They came not from the front as we had expected, but from the side and rear of our positions. Even after this long barrage, we were still taken by surprise. I had only time to shout a warning when I was hit by a bullet and passed out.

The massive 'pepperpot' bombardment had knocked all resistance out of the German defenders and they now surrendered without a struggle. The two British companies pressed on into the village. Again, all opposition melted away.

Major Loosley, who had watched the attack from his vantage point, entered the village shortly afterwards:

> The artillery bombardment was so devastating that most of the enemy were cowering in their slit trenches, numbed with shock. I had not thought that I would feel pity for the enemy, but I did when I heard the groans of the walking wounded prisoners being marched away.

With the Dorsets now in Bauchem, Captain Gilders and his forward observation crew motored into the village in their Bren carrier, known affectionately as 'Roger Dog'. The driver, Bombardier Barber, and two signallers scouted around looking for a place to set up their observation post. Barber surprised himself by unearthing two Germans who had been hiding in the centre of a stack of straw bales. They cheerfully gave themselves up and smilingly indicated a pile of eggs to the artillerymen. These tender delicacies had been protected by the two German soldiers throughout the whole of the furious bombardment and were now being passed on to someone else who would appreciate their true value. The luxury afforded a combat soldier by being in possession of a fresh egg was immeasurable. A universal treasure in a world of common misery.

By 1800 hours, Bauchem had been cleared and the road back to Gilrath opened; 182 prisoners had been taken. The Dorsets had suffered only four casualties in the attack. Patrols probed into the suburbs of Geilenkirchen to test the enemy resistance. There was none. The operation had been a complete success. As they set about consolidating their gains, the men of the battalion now looked forward to a few days' rest, expecting to be relieved the next day and go into brigade reserve at Gilrath. In this matter they were quite wrong.

Two miles to the north of Bauchem, Major Ricketts had taken over command of the 1st Worcestershires. Precious time had been lost since the colonel had been injured. The light was failing fast and Tripsrath, still over 1,000 yards ahead, was yet to be captured. The two companies earmarked for the assault, A and D, were waiting at the forming-up point for orders to come forward to the start line. To make matters worse, they were being shelled. With D Company was Private Eric Tipping:

> It had been heavy going on the move up to the forming-up point, each step we took was in mud that covered our gaiters. We were formed-up, when the enemy started to shell us. We had been ready on time to start the attack, but no orders were given to move. The delay lasted for two hours. All the while the enemy shelled us. It was almost dark before we moved off. It was most unpleasant.

Major Ricketts decided to stick to the original plan for the capture of Tripsrath, even though there would be no tank support (they were still hopelessly bogged down near the start line) and the artillery had been switched to support the Cornwalls and Dorsets in their attack. Fortunately, Ricketts was able to acquire the assurance of some help from a battery of medium guns.

A and D Companies passed through Rischden and waited on the start line just outside the village for the artillery bombardment to begin. They were to move off as soon as the shelling lifted.

At 1715 hours, the 5.5 inch medium guns began their concentration, but the Worcestershires' miseries were to continue. 'It was very seldom that our gunners made mistakes; normally they are beyond reproach,' wrote the official historian, 'but on this particular occasion they were in error.' Private Eric Tipping's D Company took the brunt of that error:

> At first, our artillery started to send a crescendo of shells crashing well to our front. I was pleased to see that the enemy was having a bit of what we had had to endure all afternoon. Then, suddenly, our shells started dropping short and within seconds were falling right in among us, forcing us to the ground and causing confusion. I was blown off of my feet and my helmet was torn off.

The blasts from the hundred pound shells caused havoc among the infantrymen, but their immediate troubles were soon over. The barrage lifted and the advance continued. Mercifully, casualties were light. The two companies easily made it to Tripsrath and were quickly joined by a third,

C Company. Resistance to the move was slight and spasmodic. The hold on the village was gradually consolidated in the gathering November darkness. The battalion had possession of Tripsrath, but its gains were not secure. The Worcestershires had formed a 1,000 yard salient into enemy territory. These three companies had no tank support, and no anti-tank guns, and the supply routes back to the rear were choked with mud and stranded vehicles. It was going to be a long night waiting for the inevitable German counter attack.

As the last light of the dull November day began to fade, the most ambitious part of the 5th Cornwalls' operation began. With Hocheid and the woods behind now in its safe hands, Colonel Taylor placed his B Company in a position to the southeast of the village occupying the high ground overlooking the hamlet of Bruggerhof and the Wurm valley. He then introduced A Company into the battle, ordering it to hold the southern end of the wood behind Hocheid. In addition, Taylor sent a patrol from this company, under Lieutenant Olding, down a small track with the intention of cutting the main road that ran northeast from Geilenkirchen. As night closed in, the platoon worked its way forward in pouring rain. The last 150 yards ran through a narrow gorge with steep banks and trees on either side. There was no opposition whatsoever. Within a very short time the platoon had established a position commanding the road into Geilenkirchen and overlooking the village of Suggerath. Unknown to the German troops in the town, their supply route, and their eventual escape route to the rear, had been closed.

Situation at 1800 hours, Saturday, 18 November
By nightfall, the British 43rd Division had captured all its objectives. Geilenkirchen was effectively surrounded. The 5th Dorsets' possession of Bauchem and the 5th Cornwalls' arrival outside Suggerath had sealed the western side of the trap. To the south, the US 405th Regiment held a solid line in front of the town. In the east, the US 334th Regiment on the high ground west of Prummern completed the great encirclement. Geilenkirchen was gradually being squeezed on three sides by a gigantic pincer movement. The intended attack by the 333rd Regiment the next morning should see the town finally fall.

On paper, the two divisions were in control of their respective sectors. In reality, there were still many pockets of enemy troops to be mopped up. The Allies had made swift gains that day. During the course of this rapidly expanding action, some open flanks between the units had become exposed. It was common knowledge that the enemy was skilful in exploiting such openings. Each battalion now sent out patrols to make contact with its neighbours and to determine the enemy's intentions. A counter attack by the German forces not only seemed likely, it appeared to be inevitable.

Chapter Eight

The First Night

Nightfall had seen Colonel Roosma move his reserve battalion, the 3rd, up to a position about 1,200 yards south of Prummern. A forward command post was established 500 yards closer to the village to facilitate command after the battalion had moved into line.

To secure the front line, the US 102nd Division's 405th Regiment, who were holding the front line when the 334th Regiment began its attack, were asked to close up with the 3rd Battalion's forward command post. In fact this did not happen and the 405th only made contact with the rear command post, leaving a 500 yard gap in the line. During the night, some enemy infantry managed to infiltrate this gap and re-occupied the 'Y' group of pillboxes. Throughout the hours of darkness, these troops continued to interfere with all American movement to the south of Prummern. The pillboxes were not cleared out again until morning.

Company F of the 2nd Battalion, was finding it hard going on the high ground to the west of Prummern. It knew little of the strength and positions of the German defenders around the new objective. The company had made little progress in the dark and by midnight had only advanced a few hundred yards. Enemy resistance consisted mainly of artillery and mortar fire, but it was enough to force the company to halt and dig in for the night, exposed though it was so far ahead of the rest of the battalion.

In the village itself, the situation was fluid in the extreme. The 1st Battalion had consolidated its positions in an orchard on the south western side, while the enemy became increasingly active on the north eastern side. His reserves, previously deterred from moving in daylight by Allied air support, were now mustering ready for a counter attack. The 1st Battalion was gradually losing its grip on the village. Some anti-tank guns were left amongst the ruined buildings, but most of the 'Railsplitters' had quit the place.

That night, in a captured German slit trench in an orchard on the outskirts of Prummern, John Mulligan and three of his buddies had collected a helmet full of green apples to eat during the night. He also had a cigar in his pocket that he had been carrying with him since having been given it in England. After

eating the green apples, he lit up the cigar and celebrated having survived his
first day in action. It was a mistake: 'I was so sick that night, that I could not
care less whether the Germans killed me or not.'

At about 0200 hours, the patrol from Company B, which had been sent out
to reconnoitre a route up to Mahogany Hill, came back and reported to
Lieutenant-Colonel Gomes. The officer in charge of the patrol had some
alarming news for him: six enemy tanks had been sighted just north of
Prummern and were moving towards the village.

Half an hour later, the German 9th Panzer Division struck. Artillery fire
from way back in the German rear began falling on Prummern. The barrage
lasted for over thirty minutes. Then the tanks moved in. The main German
counter attack against the 'Railsplitters' had begun. Infantry from the 10th
Panzer Grenadier Regiment supported by tanks of the 33rd Tank Regiment
approached the village from the north.

With no tanks of its own in Prummern to help to stem the attack, the 1st
Battalion had to depend on anti-tank guns for defence against the enemy
armour. Six German tanks in a line motored down the road and reached the
outskirts of the village. They immediately came under fire from the 'Railsplitters' Anti-Tank Company. The third of the six was knocked out and slewed
to a halt blocking the road. The leading tank charged the guns and managed to
run over one before it was knocked out by a second. The second tank in line now
broke through the defences and continued through the street until it reached
the western side of the village. Here it hit a mine and was destroyed. The
remaining three tanks retreated without penetrating the built-up area.

In the confusion, the two attacking companies of enemy infantry bypassed
the guns and dispersed among the ruined buildings. Fire now came at the
Americans from all directions. Areas of the village that had previously been
cleared were soon reclaimed by the enemy. Throughout the remainder of the
night, house to house fighting erupted all over the northern edge of the village.
No area was considered safe and sniper fire kept all movement to a minimum.
The ownership of Prummern was once again in dispute.

Richard Howland was in the village during the hours of darkness:

I was a PFC [private first class] ammunition bearer for our squad's
Browning automatic rifle; one of a handful of GIs left in Prummern that
first night. Towards dawn, after living in a foxhole in an orchard overnight,
we were told to return to the centre of the town. About twenty-five yards
from the intersection that was our destination, we stopped beside a short
wall running parallel to the street. Looking up at the intersection, we
witnessed the awful toll the sniper fire was taking on all who preceded us.
Everyone that approached the road junction was ambushed. Suddenly, a
replacement squad leader we had not seen before came up and asked us if

he should go on to the intersection, or wait it out. I couldn't believe it, he had no idea of what to do! We took a vote and decided to wait. An hour later, when nothing seemed to be happening, we moved forward again. The casualties we had witnessed were staggering.

Over on the British side of the River Wurm, it had been an interesting night for the 5th Duke of Cornwall's Light Infantry. A Company, which had cut the road into Geilenkirchen from the north-east, had not had to wait long before some of the enemy walked into its trap.

At about 1800 hours, a platoon of German infantry came marching along the main road, led by an NCO carrying a wireless set on his back, heading towards the town. They had no idea that the road had been cut. The group of enemy riflemen were marching in threes, heads down trudging wearily through the pouring rain. On either side of the road, the Cornwalls lay motionless behind their weapons, willing the enemy forward into the trap.

The British light machine guns opened up without warning. Seven of the enemy fell dead in the road. There was a scuffle and four others were taken prisoner. The remainder scattered into the night. The enemy proved to be from the 104th Panzer Grenadier Regiment, part of the 15th Panzer Grenadiers. It was evident that the 183rd Volks Grenadier Division in Geilenkirchen was being reinforced by first rate troops to stiffen the defensive role of the town.

A short while later, Lieutenant-Colonel George Taylor visited the scene. He decided to add more power to the trap and arranged for A Company to be reinforced with a 6 pounder anti-tank gun and a Vickers machine gun detachment from the 8th Middlesex, the 43rd Division's heavy machine gun battalion. Taylor feared that the previous incident would alert the enemy and the company spent the next few hours digging-in and improving the defences to the best of its ability in the dark. Mines were laid in the road and covered with leaves. Unfortunately, they were put down in pairs and this was later to prove insufficient.

The Cornwalls' next victim was a horse-drawn ammunition cart which struck one of the mines. The cart and its driver were blown sky high, but the horse trotted on alone and quickly disappeared into the darkness. A short while later another cart came ambling up the road. The unsuspecting driver halted by the damaged waggon and, duty bound, started to pick up the ammunition lying in the road. He too managed to set off a mine and was destroyed together with his cart. The horse cantered off down the road towards Geilenkirchen.

An hour later, along came another patrol, this time containing about eight men. Again the British gunfire mowed down the unsuspecting victims without warning. Five were killed instantly. The others escaped.

At around three o'clock in the morning came the night's big prize, a Tiger tank. It hit one of the mines in the road and stopped. The crew, except for the driver, jumped out and proceeded to clear the remaining explosives out of the way. A few bursts of light machine gun fire put paid to their efforts, but the small arms fire peppering the sides of the tank alerted the driver to the danger outside. The mines had not proved powerful enough to break the Tiger's massive tracks and the great monster escaped unscathed towards Kraudorf, but without the rest of its crew. They were dead.

Situation at 0600, Sunday, 19 November
The occupation of Prummern was still in dispute. The counter attack by elements of the 9th Panzer Division had been repulsed, but the enemy infiltration into the village was giving cause for concern. On the British side of the Wurm, events were passing quite peacefully. German interference with the lodgement had been slight and all the recent gains were being consolidated. The question now was: would the enemy counter attack again at dawn, as was his custom?

Chapter Nine

Consolidation

Sunday, 19 November, dawned bright and clear. Operation Clipper was twenty-four hours old. The attacks on either side of Geilenkirchen had left the town almost surrounded. The day's planned frontal assault down the river valley by the 333rd Regiment was destined to end with its final capture. Although subordinate to this main attack, the struggle for the possession of the flanks would have to continue. The Corps Commander, General Horrocks, was expecting great gains to be made that day. All units already committed to the action were ordered to resume the attack.

On the British side, the night had passed quietly. Inevitably, this brief respite ended as the first of the day's counter attacks came in with the dawn. The three companies of the 1st Worcestershires, holding the northern tip of the battlefield in the village of Tripsrath, were rudely awakened when a force of German infantry about one hundred strong came storming into their positions. A Company took the brunt of the raid. The enemy rushed the Worcestershires over open ground and immediately ran into a wall of fire from the trenches of the British. The attack withered away as suddenly as it had begun. The death toll was formidable. Daylight showed at least forty bodies in front of the forward platoon.

Although this attack had been beaten off, the village was still not clear of the enemy. D Company had found that several of them had crept back into Tripsrath during the night and were firmly positioned in the northern part of the village. In fact, all through the day, Germans were discovered in various buildings. Some were happy to surrender without a fight, while others sniped at the Worcesters and had to be evicted by force.

A little later, four Sherman tanks from the 4th/7th Royal Dragoon Guards made it through the soft ground to reinforce the Worcestershires in Tripsrath. Their stay was very short, for within two hours three of them had been knocked out by a single German. The determined enemy infantryman had stalked his prey with great courage. His hand-held weapon had knocked out all three tanks from behind; each had a hole drilled in the back armour by the panzerfaust's projectile. The fourth surviving tank was trapped, sandwiched between the wrecks of the others. Sadly, the lone German was forced to pay the supreme penalty for his bravery. He was shot dead while trying to cross the street. 'I saw his body when we entered Tripsrath, a few days later,' recalls Rex Fellows. 'It had been moved to the side of the road and was laid out on its back. His blond hair was lying down onto the ground. Much, much later, during our second stint in the village, he was still there, lying in exactly the same place. I remember thinking that his long blond hair looked as though it had grown.'

At about 1100 hours, the enemy put in another counter attack. This time the objective was Geilenkirchen. The 15th Panzer Grenadier Division attempted to get some reinforcements into the town to help those of the 183rd Volks Grenadier Division who were being attacked by the 'Railsplitters'.

The German infantry attack was supported by two self-propelled guns and two Tiger tanks. It came out of the woods to the west of Tripsrath and advanced along the axis of the road into Geilenkirchen, passing by the Worcestershires who were holed up in the village. Half a mile ahead of it lay Rischden and the Worcestershires' reserve company, B Company. Lieutenant Rex Fellows was in a trench on the northern edge of that village:

> The sound made by tank tracks, squeaking and clattering on the road surface, is a noise that you never forget. Even though they were a hell of a way away from me, I knew that they were enemy tanks. They came out from behind the woods and drove straight down the main road. I watched the leading one stop and traverse its gun around to the right. It opened up on our positions, plastering Gerry Mallinson's platoon dug-in just ahead of me on my left. One of the shells took the head and shoulders off of Mallinson's batman as he stood upright in his shallow slit trench.

B Company were now confronted by about one hundred enemy soldiers, who came out of an area of woods to the north of the village and to the west of Tripsrath. Rex Fellows watched them across the open field:

> I recollect that they were a poor lot of infantry, they did not look at all organised. It is funny the things that stick in one's mind, I remember they had their greatcoats swinging about them. They seemed to be sauntering in open formation, coming directly towards us from a distance of about five hundred yards. I told my men to hold their fire and let the enemy come within range.

The enemy tanks and infantry seemed oblivious to the British presence in Tripsrath. The exposed tanks presented broadside targets for anti-tank guns. Unfortunately, there were no anti-tank weapons in the village; it had proved too difficult a task to get them forward through the mud. The Wessexmen could only watch as the tempting targets passed on by.

Before Fellows and his men could open fire on the enemy infantry advancing towards them, the remaining companies of the Worcestershires in Tripsrath beat them to it. The resultant cross-fire caught the Germans by surprise. Hearing the fire coming from their comrades in Tripsrath, Fellows and his men also opened up on the exposed enemy. 'We really had a field day against those chaps,' he recalled. 'The German stretcher bearers were kept busy for hours and hours afterwards, picking up their dead and wounded.'

In Rischden itself, there were both anti-tank guns and Sherman tanks. These now engaged the enemy armour. Three of the German vehicles went up in flames and the screams of the men trapped in one of them could be distinctly heard above all the noise of the firing. The remaining tank bolted towards the protection of the trees.

Those of the enemy that survived retreated back into the woods for shelter. The German counter attack against the British left flank had finally petered out. There was to be no let up for the enemy troops, however, for the area they now sought shelter in had become the day's objective for another British battalion. Major-General Thomas had already decided that those woods needed clearing.

The British northern flank, and especially Tripsrath, would not be secure until the woods to the west were free of the enemy. Thomas needed clear observation to the north to prevent any further nasty surprises. In addition, the next phase of the operation called for an attack on the two villages of Straeten and Waldenrath by 130 Brigade, and possession of the woods was essential before the assault could begin. He therefore decided that the 5th Dorsets should be relieved of the occupation of Bauchem by the 4th Somerset Light Infantry, so that the battalion could advance northwards and clear the wooded area.

Over to the right of Tripsrath was another long wood that stretched from the village of Hocheid north eastwards to the hamlet of Hoven. Thomas also wanted this wood cleared. He ordered Lieutenant-Colonel Borradaile to send his 7th Somerset Light Infantry across from its base in Niederheide and advance through this forest to the northern edge. This movement would bring his forces into a straight line abreast of the Americans on the other side of the River Wurm. Tripsrath could then form a secure anchor to XXX Corps' northern flank, buttressed by an entrenched battalion on either side.

The 5th Dorsets in Bauchem had been expecting to be relieved and sent into reserve after its attack on the village the day before. Arrangements for the relief were already in hand when Brigadier Coad arrived at battalion headquarters with the news of General Thomas's change of plans. The brigadier told Lieutenant-Colonel Venour that prompt action was required and the woods must be cleared that day.

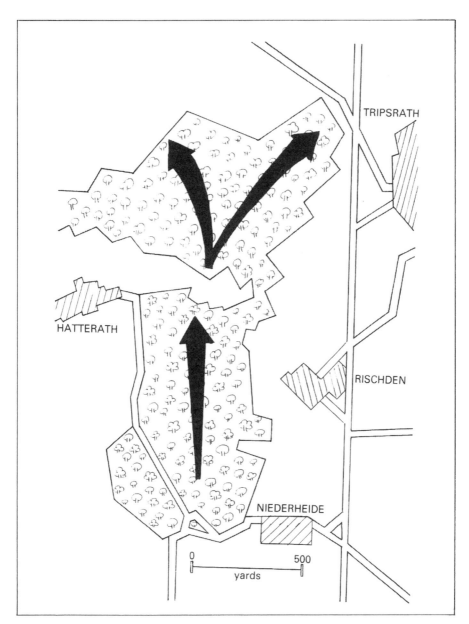

Map 5: The 5th Dorsets Attack Through The Woods.

At 1345 hours, the 5th Dorsets set off towards its new objective. Assisted by a squadron of Sherman tanks from the 13th/18th Royal Hussars, the infantry crossed the open ground under a cover of a smoke screen laid by the mortars. Away to the right, in the village of Niederheide, the men of the 7th Somersets could be seen beginning their move eastwards towards the other set of woods to be cleared that day.

Up near the front of the 5th Dorsets' attack was a forward observation crew from the 112th Field Artillery Royal Artillery. Bombardier Ron Barber was in a carrier just behind the Dorsets and alongside the tanks of the 13th/18th Royal Hussars as they swept across the muddy fields towards the line of trees. He saw an enemy soldier come running out of the woods with his hands up yelling at the top of his voice. The tank next to Barber riddled the German with bullets. 'My troop commander blew his top at this atrocity, but the response from the tank was negative.' On this sombre note the Dorsets entered the dark woods.

The battalion advanced on a two-company front; C on the right, and A on the left. B and D Companies followed closely behind. The axis for the move was the main track that ran northwards through the forest. The woods being cleared were split into two distinct halves, with a wide clearing separating them roughly on a line with the village of Rischden. The going was extremely heavy. Continual rain from the preceding weeks had softened the ground so much that any movement churned the surface into the consistency of blancmange. Mud was everywhere and soon everything became covered in slime.

All movement slowed to a crawl; vehicles slithered aimlessly on the wet track. The infantry on either side shuffled slowly forward, easing one foot in front of the other through the thick mire. It took three hours to cover the first mile.

Fortunately, all went well with no sign of an enemy presence in the wood. The open space was reached and the ground ahead surveyed. Nothing could be seen. The way looked clear and the Dorsets continued the advance, but there was trouble ahead. The 15th Panzer Grenadiers were waiting in the trees on the far side of the clearing. As the leading companies moved across the clear ground, the Germans opened up on the Dorsetmen.

Mortar and machine gun fire cut a swath through the exposed British infantry. Men fell dead all along the line. Both companies were forced back into the southern section of the woods. Mortar fire followed their retreat and gave them good incentive to get below ground as soon as possible. To add to their discomfort, the Germans called up artillery support and the whole area was transformed into a nightmare of crashing trees and red hot splinters of steel. Casualties were horrific. The Dorsets had walked into a carefully prepared trap. The advance shuddered to an abrupt halt.

Most of the supporting vehicles had become bogged down in the heavy going. The Hussar's tanks were stuck back near the entrance to the woods. There were no heavy weapons available to support the Dorsets; the battalion was on its own.

Colonel Venour ordered D Company to try to outflank the enemy by moving round to the left and into a section of the wood that protruded into the western part of the clearing. The position would provide D Company with an excellent opportunity to subject the enemy to enfilade and protect the remainder of the battalion as it crossed the open ground. The company set out on its flanking movement, but the treacherous conditions and enemy fire made progress slow. By this time, it was late afternoon and the light was already fading fast. Colonel Venour quickly realised that it would soon be too dark for this objective to be gained that night and ordered D Company to dig in where it was. He also told the other companies to wait until it was completely dark and then withdraw to a more favourable position, back from the forward edge of the wood. While the shells continued to crash around them, the 5th Dorsets settled down for an uncomfortable night in the wet forest.

The 7th Somerset Light Infantry's attack on Hocheid Wood fared little better than the 5th Dorsets' attack. There was no possibility of tank support, for the ground was too heavy for them to get forward. The Somersets therefore attacked with the support of an artillery barrage.

Among the leading troops was Sergeant Dan Robertson. 'As we lined up on the start line prior to the advance', he remembers, 'the artillery fired a "block concentration" into the woods. When we reached the line of trees, the barrage lifted three hundred yards and we plunged into the forest.'

The battalion was blasted through the woods with the artillery concentration lifting one hundred yards every five minutes. Within an hour, the two leading companies had reached their first objective and held the southern part of Hocheid Wood. Again the wood under attack was split into two with a clearing between the northern and southern parts. The Somersets halted in front of the clearing. Very soon, the expected enemy counter fire started to come whistling over. Robertson remembers the scene:

We had dug in as quickly as possible and were somewhat surprised when we received orders not to cover our fighting slit trenches in case of a quick enemy counter attack. Jerry had the wood well and truly 'zeroed in' and shelled and mortared us incessantly. It was raining heavily in more ways than one! The air burst effect of German mortar bombs and artillery fire literally rained shrapnel down on us. This continued until darkness fell.

The other battalion of the British 43rd Division in action that day was the 5th Duke of Cornwall's Light Infantry. It was still holding its positions overlooking the northern escape route out of Geilenkirchen. For the Cornishmen, it was a quiet day. The only thing to spoil the infantry's mood was the lack of a hot meal. The battalion's transport had become bogged down in the mud near Hocheid and there was little likelihood of getting supplies through before nightfall.

On the lighter side, A Company's ranks had been swelled by two unexpected newcomers – the horses from the ill-fated ammunition waggons that had been knocked out during the ambush the previous night. They grazed contentedly in the field behind the company's line, expertly dodging the mortar and artillery concentrations that fell about them from both sides.

The Cornwalls did not move that day. They remained guarding the road and waiting for the Americans to press home their attack on Geilenkirchen. The 'Railsplitters' were expected to come marching out of the town sometime later that morning, if all went well.

While the British 43rd Division was consolidating its side of the battlefield that Sunday morning, the American 334th Regiment was doing the same on the eastern flank. Colonel Roosma had committed all three of his battalions in the struggle for Prummern and the surrounding area. The 1st and 3rd Battalions were trying to clear Prummern and get the attack on Mahogany Hill started, while the 2nd Battalion moved north-eastwards to command the high ground between the village and Suggerath. Both objectives proved to be formidable and enemy resistance had increased beyond all measure since the previous day. Rapid gains were things of the past. The 334th Regiment would now have to fight bitterly for every new foot of German soil it attempted to capture.

Lieutenant-Colonel Gomes once again ordered his battalion to reoccupy Prummern. The village had to be cleared finally of all enemy troops to be ready for the 3rd Battalion's attack on Mahogany Hill at 1100 hours. The 1st Battalion was then to launch its own attack on the area south of Beeck.

John Mulligan was a private in Company A. The company had spent an uncomfortable night in a waterlogged slit trench sited in an orchard on the eastern edge of the village. Just after dawn, the men were roused from their foxholes and told to get ready to move out. As the company was forming up on the road, Mulligan noticed that he had left his raincoat in his foxhole. He jumped back into the hole to get it and called Sergeant Pfeiffer to come down and help him stuff the raincoat in the back of the gunbelt that he was wearing. While he was doing this, the enemy brought down an artillery barrage on the orchard. Mulligan and Pfeiffer pressed themselves deep into the hole so as to escape the effects of the shells bursting in the trees. When the shelling ceased, they climbed out of the trench to find the area covered with bodies. Twenty-two people were lost in the barrage. The entire company had been caught in the open as it moved out of the orchard.

The remainder of Company A had scattered during the bombardment and had moved off down the road. Mulligan and Pfeiffer set out to catch up with it. They took a wrong turning and soon found themselves lost. Then the shelling started up again. It was the worst shelling of the battle so far. It seemed as though every gun in the German Army was zeroed in on Prummern and the surrounding area. Mulligan remembers lying in deep tank tracks in the mud, listening to the shrapnel whistling overhead, and praying like never before.

Later the two men came across some British tanks from the Sherwood Rangers. Mulligan asked where Company A had gone, but the tank commander said he did not know. 'We stayed with them for a long while until our company was finally located,' Mulligan recalled, adding: 'I remember the tank crew, directing artillery fire with their hatches open. When a shell landed close by they would move the tank forward. When the next shell hit they would move the tank back again. Nothing seemed to bother them.'

The 1st Battalion soon found that trying to retake Prummern was not going to be as easy as the first attempt had been the day before. The calibre of the Germans defending the village had improved. The 'Railsplitters' found that elements of the 9th Panzer Division had taken up residence among the buildings. Infantry from the 10th Panzer Grenadier Regiment had infiltrated the village during the night, in order to stiffen the resolve of the Volks Grenadiers who were defending Prummern.

Movement through the buildings was slow and dangerous. Each house in turn had to be cleared by the GIs. Close quarters gun battles broke out all over the village. Hand to hand fighting spilled over from one building into another. It was a nightmare. No one could tell which was the front and which was the rear. The Germans were everywhere.

At 1100 hours, Colonel Roosma committed the 3rd Battalion. Company I moved into the eastern side of Prummern to prepare a sound base for the remainder of the battalion to attack through. It, too, met fierce resistance. A whole German company barred its way. Once again, the 'Railsplitters' were involved in hand to hand fighting. It was a grim indoctrination into battle for the 3rd Battalion. Company K was following closely behind and now lent its weight to the firefight. Slowly the enemy were overcome and the eastern side of Prummern was cleared sufficiently for the main attack to begin, albeit several hours late.

At 1550 hours, the massed guns of XXX Corps concentrated their fire on Mahogany Hill and the ground to the north. The artillery barrage was laid on the 3rd Battalion's objective for ten minutes and then lifted and rolled towards the village of Beeck. Behind the deluge, the two leading companies began their attack.

The 1st Battalion should have been attacking at the same time on the left, but it had been halted by a tremendous German artillery concentration and had been forced to dig in. The battalion had stopped in a most unhealthy position, right beneath the enemy on the top of Mahogany Hill. The Germans overlooked its every move.

Meanwhile, the 3rd Battalion attacked alone. It had been ordered to: 'Move forward if possible, and to exploit the potency of the barrage'. Companies I and K tried, but they, too, were under the watchful eyes of the Germans on the high ground. After a few hundred yards, the infantrymen were halted.

Company L now entered the fray and swung around the right of the other two companies. It was no use; all open movement drew more artillery fire. The German positions on the high ground were so strong that continuation was impossible. The 3rd Battalion called a halt to the attack and secured itself positions for the night away from enemy observation. Mahogany Hill remained untouched.

Earlier that day, the 2nd Battalion of the 334th Regiment was set to continue its progress towards Beeck. It had spent the night on the high ground to the west of Prummern. The advance was a resumption of the move ordered the evening before by Brigadier-General Bolling. Its objective was the area to the north-east above the village of Wurm. The route was to take it along the ridge that overlooked Suggerath.

As promised, Major Peter Selerie brought his squadron of the Sherwood Rangers back up to the 2nd Battalion to support the advance. 'Apparently,' recalls Major Selerie, 'they had been ordered to push one company forward as night fell. Since then, they had received no signal from it. The battalion commander was naturally anxious to establish what had happened. I offered to go forward in the direction taken by the missing company with B Squadron.'

The armour advanced with one troop, consisting of three tanks as a vanguard, across the open ground. Selerie followed just to the rear of them in his squadron headquarters' tank, together with a company of protecting infantry.

The isolated company, Company F, was pinned down about four hundred yards in front of the rest of the battalion, on an exposed slope unable to move. The company was caught in the cross-fire from several pillboxes. Daylight had made its very existence most precarious. No open movement was possible. The Germans in the concrete emplacements punished anyone foolish enough to show himself.

Like cavalry galloping forward in an old western film, the Sherwood Rangers came to the rescue. The pillboxes were strafed with machine gun and high explosive fire from the tanks. This counter fire gave the besieged company some respite from its continual harassment.

Halting towards the top of a slight rise, the accompanying infantry company commander signalled to Major Selerie that he wanted to speak to him:

> I took off my headphones and called out to him to get up on the rear of the tank so that we could talk above the roar of the engine. We exchanged a few words and it was apparent that our intervention was enabling the lost company to withdraw and rejoin the remainder of the battalion. At this moment we were engaged by German tanks in hull down positions, as well as by some anti-tank guns.

Two tanks in the leading troops were hit immediately and shortly afterwards the third. Selerie's tank was next. Within seconds, the squadron leader's Sherman was struck twice by armour-piercing shells, one of them penetrating the turret. Those of the crew who were able to do so baled out quickly. The major was thrown out of his turret by his radio operator and gunner. He was badly injured:

> I regained consciousness to find high explosive rounds bursting around me. Oddly enough, my brain must have ceased recording the position of my limbs precisely when I was hit. I still thought that my right arm was above my head, when in reality it was lying shattered, so to speak, by my side. What was more alarming was that I had a bad wound in the upper part of my right leg from which I was losing copious amounts of blood. With my good arm I tried to jam as much of my battle dress slacks as possible into the hole. The shelling was increasing in intensity and I therefore tried to crawl away from the vicinity of the burning tanks. With only one allegedly good arm (the one in which I had been wounded in Normandy) and one good leg, the progress was somewhat slow!

The 2nd Battalion spent the rest of that day trying to reach the objective. It proved to be impossible. There was no cover on the high ground and the Germans had all the advantages. Enemy positions covered every approach. Dug-in tanks and camouflaged anti-tank guns controlled each projecting slope and re-entrant. Every time any tank or infantryman crested a hill, they found themselves silhouetted against the skyline and were duly chastised by enemy fire. Not surprisingly, casualties were high and progress slow. George Green was with Company E during the advance that day:

> I was a rifle grenadier. That is, I had a grenade launcher attached to my rifle in order to lob grenades at tanks, but I traded this monster for a regular rifle the first chance I had. We soon learned that to survive you had to move fast and stay low. We threw away, or lost, most of our equipment. I eventually had only a rusty spoon left to eat with. I had dumped luxuries like my mess kit as soon as I could, so that I was able to carry more useful things like grenades and ammunition.

The high casualty rate meant that there were great opportunities for advancement. 'Dead man's boots' Green called it. 'Almost every day you could move up in rank or responsibility, if you happened to survive. After the first day of combat, we never saw an officer higher than a first lieutenant up at the front with us.'

Situation at 1800 hours, Sunday, 19 November
On the British side of the battlefield, slight gains had been made in the two woods adjacent to Tripsrath. The 5th Dorsets had penetrated the southern half of its wood, but then had been stopped dead by strong enemy resistance. Much the same had happened to the 7th Somersets in the woods to the north of Hocheid. The southern part of the wood was captured, but the enemy were strong in the northern end. In between, the 1st Worcestershires still held the village of Tripsrath and had beaten off two determined German counter attacks. The troops of the 5th Duke of Cornwall's Light Infantry held the southern flank of the British sector and were waiting for the Americans to meet up with them from the direction of Geilenkirchen.

The four British battalions were all in strong positions to deal with any enemy attempts to win back lost ground. By now, they had all stopped and had consolidated the day's small gains. Overlooking them from the high ground on the far side of the River Wurm, were the heavy guns of the Siegfried Line. It was not going to be a quiet night.

On the American side of the front, the 334th Regiment had made little progress that day. The 1st and 3rd Battalions had recaptured Prummern, but had advanced no more than a few hundred yards north-east of the village. Their positions were under perfect observation from the enemy on Mahogany Hill. The 2nd Battalion had fared even worse. It had advanced only a few hundred yards, and that small gain was made at great cost.

The actions that day on either side of Geilenkirchen had not been XXX Corps' only contact with the enemy. Earlier that morning, the 333rd Regiment had put Phase 2 of Operation Clipper into effect: Geilenkirchen itself had been attacked, head on, from the south.

Company E advanced in broad daylight over open fields. The British tanks assigned to it were having some difficulty manoeuvring in the thick mud and were delayed at the start. The company moved out with no protection to advance behind. After what seemed just a few yards, the riflemen became pinned down by some accurate enemy shelling. The infantry took cover where they could find it, but it was hopeless. The open ground made the men sitting ducks. The whole company went to ground and stayed put for the rest of the day.

George Green scratched a shallow foxhole for himself as best he could, all the while trying to keep as low a profile as possible.

The shelling just went on and on, we could not move either forward or backwards. The whole company was stuck in the same spot for most of the day. My friend, PFC Hart, only an arm's length away from me was decapitated by shrapnel. By the end of the day we were all pretty tired and hungry. You cannot imagine how the absence of food and water can emerge as such desperate realities in a situation like that. I reached over to Hart, wiped the blood off of his rations and ate them. I also drank the water out of his canteen. Looking at his mangled body, I recalled the poignant final visit his father had paid on him just before we left camp.

Chapter Ten

Geilenkirchen

With the British in the villages to the west of Geilenkirchen and the American 334th Regiment on the high ground to the east, the enemy-held town had taken on the shape of a thin salient surrounded by Allied held territory. Overlooked on three sides, the German position in the town had become untenable. The 183rd Volks Grenadier Division should have attempted a breakout to the north and safety early on 19 November. Indeed, its Commander, Generalleutnant Wolfgang Lange was requesting permission to do just that, but his new corps commander, General Blumentritt, had other ideas. Voluntary withdrawal was an anathema to the German High Command. The 1st Battalion of the German 343rd Infantry Regiment, was ordered to remain in Geilenkirchen and defend the town. To help them, a counter attack was being organised by the 15th Panzer Grenadier Division, who had recently arrived in the area.

A glance at the map of the German Westwall fortifications around Geilenkirchen shows that the main fixed defences follow the line of hills to the east of the River Wurm. This great belt of pillboxes and bunkers was positioned to make the best use of the undulating high ground overlooking the river valley. On the flat land to the west, the British 43rd Division was beginning to feel the effects of having the enemy overlooking them from the emplacements of the Siegfried Line. Artillery fire on a scale that it had not witnessed for many months was now descending on the scattered villages so recently captured.

However, the main armament of these pillboxes was not field guns firing shells but machine guns firing bullets. The defences were designed to stop the infantry at close quarters by making any approach to the bunkers deadly. The line of pillboxes east of Geilenkirchen formed a long fortified belt which stretched up the Wurm Valley for miles. Normal tactics would suggest that an attack could be expected to approach these fixed defences from the front, with the assault hoping to penetrate the line quickly and get behind the emplacements. To achieve this breakthrough, around a dozen pillboxes would have to be taken at the most. Once the fixed defences were eliminated, the infantry could then fan out in the rear.

Early on the morning of Sunday, 19 November 1944, the American 333rd Regiment was preparing for the assault on Geilenkirchen. The 84th Division's Field Order No 4, required the 333rd to attack at 0700 hours, clear the Wurm Valley southwest of Geilenkirchen and then the town itself. However, the previous day, General Horrocks had changed his plans and had decided to combine together several phases of Operation Clipper. He now wanted the British 43rd Division to resume its attack north eastwards and to keep abreast of the 334th's attack on Beeck on the opposite side of the River Wurm. In the centre, Horrocks ordered the 333rd Regiment to push on with its attack right up the river valley to seize successively, Geilenkirchen, Suggerath, Mullendorf and finally the village of Wurm. The effect would be to bring the whole of XXX Corps' front up together in line and remove any exposed flanks.

The result of this new order would mean that the 333rd Regiment would now be attacking along the length of the Siegfried Line emplacements to get to Wurm. It was being asked to assault and capture one pillbox after another, on one of the strongest sections of Hitler's formidable Westwall. Between the start line south of Geilenkirchen and the 333rd's final objective, the village of Wurm, there were seventy-two such pillboxes. This new order would commit the regiment to an advance along one of the most heavily fortified valleys in Germany. Casualties were bound to be high.

Colonel Timothy Pedley Jr, Commander of the 333rd Regiment, decided to use his 1st Battalion to carry out the assault on Geilenkirchen. The Commander of the 1st Battalion, Lieutenant-Colonel Thomas Woodyard, in turn, selected Companies A and B to launch the attack.

The town of Geilenkirchen is divided by the River Wurm, with the majority of the built up area on the western side. Woodyard chose to use the river as a boundary between his two units, with Company A on the left and Company B on the right, the eastern, side of the Wurm.

The plan of attack was fairly simple. The assault was to be preceded by an artillery barrage from massed American and British artillery. At 0700 hours, the two companies would move off, supported by British tanks. On paper, Company A had the hardest task, having to attack through the centre of the town and most of the buildings, while Company B had more open ground and the use of the main Aachen-Monchengladbach railway line to advance along. In consequence, it was expected to make the better progress and Colonel Woodyard chose to accompany this right hand unit during the assault. Company C was ordered to follow closely behind, ready to exploit any breakthrough on this side of the valley.

When Company A marched out of Frelenberg in a long column on the road towards Geilenkirchen, it was still dark. The muzzle flashes of the artillery and the thunder of the big guns gave the men some assurance that they were being

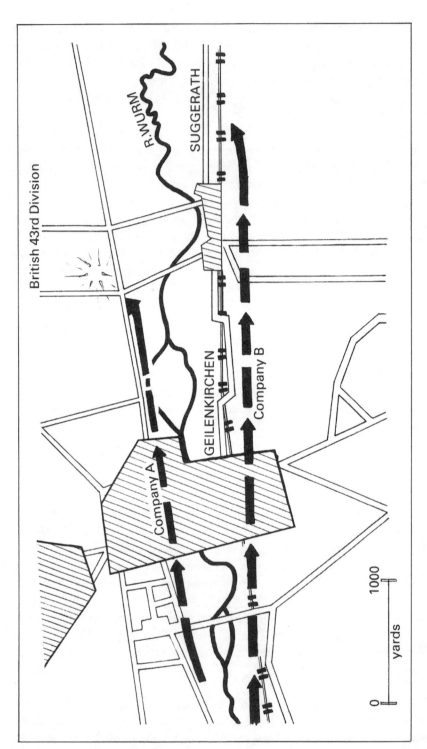

Map 6: The 333rd Regiment's Attack on Geilenkirchen.

well supported. Hearing very little German counter fire as he trudged along the road, Private John J. O'Malley was led to believe that the attack might not be so difficult after all.

> While our company officers may have been given a good bit more information about the geography, fortifications and disposition of the enemy, we were told very little about what was to come. We did, however, know that we would be supported by British tanks of the Sherwood Rangers Regiment, and, although I did not envy the tank crews who would have to slug it out in American M4 Sherman tanks against far superior German armour, their very name, 'Sherwood Rangers', seemed to give them a dash of bravado which couldn't but help our morale.

At 0700 hours, the operation to eliminate the Geilenkirchen salient began. From a start line 500 yards south of the town, the 1st Battalion moved off. Company B ran into the enemy as soon as the attack started. It had just entered a small wooded area in the loop of the Immendorf railway line, when about six Germans walked out of a trench and gave themselves up. The company's first casualties were suffered in the same wood, as a result of some anti-personnel mines. Wooden schu mines, unable to be detected by normal means, were buried among the trees and the advancing infantry walked right into the minefield. Two men were killed and another was injured before the situation was sorted out.

After a short hold-up while a path was cleared, the company moved off once again. From then on it was easy going. Company B made the eastern side of the town against little resistance. By 0900 hours, it was clearing the buildings near the middle of Geilenkirchen. Close behind came Company C.

Joe Garcia was in the centre of Company C as it advanced in single columns along either side of the railway line towards the town. As the company had reached the outskirts of the town, Garcia could hear the word 'medic' being passed down the line.

> Our platoon medic hurried forward along the middle of the railroad track, holding his medical bags on each side as he ran. A short while later he came back, his eyes as big as silver dollars. All he could say was, 'He's dead.' A scout from Company B ahead of us had been hit by a sniper. We all looked at each other and felt a sinking feeling in our stomachs.

Meanwhile, Company A was moving up on the left. At first, it was able to keep abreast of Company B. There was little artillery or mortar fire to interfere with the advance and enemy resistance was slight. After a few hundred yards the company stumbled across two pillboxes that had never been spotted before.

This caused some delay on the extreme left, but the remainder of the company pressed on.

The company's left flank was giving some cause for concern. The British were known to be somewhere out there on that side, but continuous patrols failed to make any contact with them. To protect itself, Company A was forced to use more flank protection than had been earlier envisaged. This slowed up the advance and thinned out the attack. However, things were still going quite well, for the enemy had yet to put in an appearance.

On the extreme right flank of the Company, John O'Malley was advancing along the left bank of the River Wurm in the company of Jonathan L. White Jr. During the short time he had known him, O'Malley had come to have a high regard for his friend:

> Jonathan came from the small town of Erwin, deep in the eastern mountains of Tennessee. He was known to us as 'Junior' and was the squad's automatic rifleman. Junior never seemed to get rattled; he would fire his Browning Automatic Rifle at anything and everything he was ordered to, and occasionally without any orders. He would fire the BAR in the same way he would have shot at squirrels back home in Tennessee. To me, he personified the 'Tennessee Volunteer'; a sandy haired, fair skinned, soft spoken, unemotional, God fearing type of man, who could always be relied on. Junior was a few years older than me, and I had great confidence in him on the battlefield.

This left side of the company's advance had met no opposition whatsoever. The warm winter sun made the going uncomfortable for the 3rd Platoon, and O'Malley and his companion ducked down into a shell hole for a rest and a cigarette. No sooner had they sat down when they heard the characteristic snapping noise of machine gun bullets.

Jonathan White looked across the meadow towards Geilenkirchen and a row of imposing brick houses that lined the road about a hundred yards to their left. He then calmly said, 'John, I think we are being fired upon.' O'Malley recalls the conversation:

> I immediately questioned his judgement, for I found it impossible to believe that soldiers with the reputation of the German army could have intended the two of us as targets and yet managed to miss us from a distance of only a few hundred yards. I told Junior he was wrong and that we were hearing Company D's machine guns firing in support of our attack. But Junior was not convinced by my analysis of the situation. 'John,' he said in his soft Tennessee drawl, 'I reckon that there are

Brigadier-General Alexander Bolling, Commander of the US 84th ('Railsplitters') Division. Bolling had served with the US 4th Infantry Division during the First World War in France, where he won the Distinguished Service Cross. After the Second World War he was appointed Lieutenant-General in command of US Third Army and later became Chief of Army Intelligence. (*US National Archives*)

Major-General Gwilym Ivor Thomas, Commander of the 43rd (Wessex) Division. Thomas served with the Royal Artillery in France during the First World War, winning the Distinguished Service Order and Military Cross and Bar. After the Second World War he rose to the rank of full general and became the Quartermaster-General. (*Pat Spencer Moore*)

The ruins of Geilenkirchen from the air before its capture by the 'Railsplitters' in November 1944. The town had been under intermittent shell fire from American troops since their arrival in the area in September. (*IWM*)

Part of the defences of the Siegfried Line. Anti-tank obstacles zigzag across the ground near Geilenkirchen in 1944. (*Norbert Rosin*)

The same stretch of the Siegfried defences today. (*Norbert Rosin*)

Left to right: Lieutenant-General Brian Horrocks, Commander of the British XXX Corps, Field Marshal Montgomery, Commander of the 21st British Army Group, and Major-General Thomas, Commander of the 43rd (Wessex) Division. (*IWM*)

Major-General Thomas motoring near the German border, close to Teveren. From the rear seat his ADC, Pat Spencer Moore, looks nonchalantly at the cameraman as the scout car speeds past, taking the general up to the front line. (*IWM*)

British troops advancing through Gilrath up to the start line at the beginning of the battle. (*Willi Offermann*)

The same location at Gilrath today. (*Norbert Rosin*)

A knocked-out German Panther tank is hauled back through Geilenkirchen down Jülicher Str. by American engineers. (*US National Archives*)

British troops from the 5th Dorsets clear houses in Bauchem during their attack on the village on the opening day of the battle. (*IWM*)

American troops moving through Geilenkirchen during the mopping-up of the town. Most of the enemy resistance had been light. The real problems lay just to the north of the built-up area. (*IWM*)

Tanks of the Sherwood Rangers move up with the American infantry. The British Sherman tanks found the going difficult once off the roads. Enemy minefields took a heavy toll of their numbers. (*IWM*)

British troops escort prisoners to the rear. Most of the enemy resistance to the initial attacks was sporadic and light. (*IWM*)

Sherwood Rangers support Company A of the 'Railsplitters' during their attack northwards along Heinsberger Str. in Geilenkirchen towards Randerath. (*IWM*)

British troops make sure there is no further enemy resistance from this German dug-out during their attack on Tripsrath. (*IWM*)

American troops advance up to the start line. The 'Railsplitters' move forward along the muddy roads to prepare for their first attack of the war. (*IWM*)

American engineers blow up a German strongpoint near Geilenkirchen to prevent the enemy reoccupying the position. (*US National Archives*)

On its way up to the front, a British tanks pauses outside a house in Gilrath. (*Willi Offermann*)

The same house today. (*Norbert Rosin*)

American troops escort German prisoners through Geilenkirchen. (*US National Archives*)

The same point along Martin-Heyden-Str. today. (*Norbert Rosin*)

American infantry moving through Immendorf towards Geilenkirchen past a knocked-out German Panther tank. (*US National Archives*)

Transport bogged down on the plateau near Prummern. The thick mud made any journey across open ground very hazardous. Enemy artillery had the co-ordinates of any significant point on the barren landscape. Any hesitation was punished by shellfire. (*IWM*)

A crew member from a Sherman tank of the 4th/7th Dragoon Guards negotiates the muddy ground to get some water for a brew of tea. One of the lasting memories of any of the Americans who had contact with British troops was 'the Limeys' continual need to stop and drink tea'. (*IWM*)

The same location in Palenberg today. (*Norbert Rosin*)

German prisoners are escorted back through Übach to a prisoner-of-war cage. (*US National Archives*)

The same location today. (*Norbert Rosin*)

American infantry talking with a British sergeant in the centre of Geilenkirchen after the town's capture. (*US National Archives*)

Brigadier Essame (left), Commander of the British 214 Brigade, talks to Lieutenant-Colonel Osborne Smith, Commander of the 1st Worcestershire Regiment, prior to the attack on Rischden and Tripsrath. (*IWM*)

The underground command post of Brigadier Essame's 214 Brigade during the battle. (*Willi Offermann*)

A Sherman tank of the Sherwood Rangers Yeomanry fires its machine gun at an enemy strongpoint while assisting Company A in its attack on Geilenkirchen. (*IWM*)

The area around the hospital in Geilenkirchen as it is today. (*Norbert Rosin*)

Stretcher bearers bringing in one of the infantry wounded in the attack on Beeck. Casualties were high during the 405th Regiment's assault on the village. (*US National Archives*)

American infantry dug-in on a hill outside Geilenkirchen. Whenever troops halted, it was vital to get below ground as soon as possible to escape the inevitable enemy shelling. (*US National Archives*)

American mortars support yet another attack towards Beeck from their positions alongside an orchard in Prummern. (*US National Archives*)

American troops dug-in alongside the pillbox near the crossroads outside Prummern that had caused so much trouble during the early attempts to advance out of the village. (The emplacement had been blown up by engineers immediately after its capture.) (*IWM*)

American troops advance across open ground near Beeck. There was little cover for the troops once the shelling began. (*US National Archives*)

American infantry moving through the underpass at Suggerath. This underpass was later demolished to allow tanks to pass underneath the railway line and on to the high ground to the east of the village. (*US National Archives*)

The top brass plan the next battle. Major-General Frank Keating (right), Commander of the 102nd (Ozark) Division, demonstrates how his men will attack across the River Roer in early 1945. Watching are the senior American commanders in the area. Left to right: Major-General Raymond McLain, Commander of the US XIX Corps; Major-General Alvan Gillem, Commander of the US XIII Corps; Lieutenant-General Bill Simpson, Commander of the US 9th Army; and General Omar Bradley, Commander of the US 12th Army Group. The 84th ('Railsplitters') Division also crossed the River Roer in this battle. (*US National Archives*)

Germans in that house over yonder (pointing) and they are firing at us.' I looked but saw nothing unusual.

The 3rd Platoon was coming under machine gun and sniper fire from the edge of the town. It was time for the platoon to start its initiation into the heat of battle. The entire platoon was ordered to close up on the houses and the road. The house from which the Germans had been firing at O'Malley was across the road and the platoon approached it behind the protection given by the walls of a nearby building.

O'Malley firmly resolved to pay much closer heed to Junior's observations in the days ahead, as they ducked down behind some cover and studied the house. Every now and then one or two of the platoon would peer cautiously around the corner and Junior would fire bursts from his BAR with the quiet confidence which he must have felt from having been proved right. They knew, however, that small arms fire from their position would cause little more than harassment and they strongly recommended to Junior that he save his ammunition. He followed their advice and they sat around resting and awaited further developments.

Not long afterwards, they knew that the situation would soon be well in hand when they heard the roar of Sherman tanks approaching. The Sherwood Rangers came clanking up the road in their armour. The first tank stopped in front of the house, swung its turret around and fired a cannon round into the wall surrounding the building, blowing a large hole in it. This seemed to provide the proper incentive for the German troops inside to surrender. Before a second round was fired, a white handkerchief at the end of a stick appeared at the front door. Someone shouted at them to come out with their hands up and, as soon as they did so, they were sent to the rear.

O'Malley's platoon now continued on its way again towards the centre of the town, crossing one garden fence after another and all the while keeping a sharp eye out for snipers. The tanks moved off down the road, firing high explosive shells into every house and building. The rest of the infantry followed close behind, mopping up any of the enemy who did not surrender or take flight.

The Commander of the 84th Division, Brigadier-General Alexander Bolling, spent the morning at the 333rd's Regimental Command Post in Zroeibruggen. He watched the progress of the battle with concern. His division was very much the newcomer to the battlefield and he was witnessing the 333rd Regiment's first attack. His right flank was worrying him. Although he had troops in Prummern, they had been counter attacked in the night and were making slow progress in recapturing the village. At 0945 hours, when Company B had reached the centre of the town, Bolling was heard to say: 'Our flank is sort of out in the breeze now.'

His doubts persisted. At 1000 hours, he claimed: 'Our chief concern at this point is our right flank. The 2nd Armored Division has advanced only to Immendorf-Apweiler. I have pushed a salient up the river valley and they haven't advanced.'

Bolling was clearly concerned that the German 15th Panzer Grenadier Division had become active in that area and was likely to move against the 'Rail-splitters' recent gains at any time. Bolling saw this eastern flank as being his weakest point. Since the 3rd Battalion of the 334th Regiment had been committed in Prummern, a sizeable area south of the village between there and Immendorf was wide open. Bolling expected the enemy counter attack to be made there.

He therefore decided to bring extra resources in to play. He explained: 'The 405th Infantry Regiment of the 102nd Division has just been attached to me by the Army Commander and I intend to use its 2nd Battalion west of Immendorf, ready to meet any thrust from the right flank. I'll get in behind them if they hit me there. We'll hold that salient.' Accordingly, the 2nd Battalion of the 405th Infantry Regiment – the divisional reserve – was moved into a position to the left of Immendorf to block a German counter attack.

The 405th were from the US 102nd Division, commanded by Major General Frank Keating. The 102nd was known as the 'Ozark Division'. It originated from the states of Missouri and Arkansas, the Ozark region. The name went back to the days when the French first settled the area. They found it inhabited by Indians who were very proficient with the bow and arrow, and therefore called the entire region, 'Terre Aux Arcs,' or 'Bow Country', 'Ozark', is the Americanisation of 'aux arcs'. The Divisional insignia combined a golden 'O' and 'Z' on a circular blue background.

As Company A reached the centre of Geilenkirchen, they started receiving automatic weapons fire again. One by one, the buildings were cleared. In the 3rd Platoon, O'Malley and his squad were assigned a row of houses to check out. The men ran from one to another, thoroughly searching each one, floor by floor, room by room. Up ahead of him, O'Malley watched as someone lobbed a grenade into a cellar. Enemy troops were thought to be sheltering inside. A few moments later, just as he was passing the front door of the building, two German soldiers stumbled out and up the steps, almost colliding with him. One man was supporting the other who was bleeding profusely from a wound in his side. Since the two Germans were unarmed, they were left alone to find their own way back to the rear. The squad continued into the next building. No more enemy were found in the row of buildings and O'Malley and the others walked back to the main square. On the way, he saw the wounded German soldier sprawled out on the sidewalk, dead.

Company A's task was to move through Geilenkirchen as quickly as possible. Speed was everything; it was essential that progress up the river valley should continue that day. The final clearing of the town was to be left for follow-up troops.

At around 1430 hours, Company A formed up in the town square to receive orders for the next move. It had been told that the final mopping up of Geilenkirchen was to be completed by Company K from the 3rd Battalion. Company A was directed to move out of the town along the road that led to Randerath. This would take them along the axis that separated the US 84th Division and the British 43rd Division.

Over the other side of the River Wurm, Company B was well ahead of its sister company back in Geilenkirchen. It had made very good progress during its attack and had passed through the town and on up the valley. During its movement through the built-up area, the only real difficulty it encountered was with occasional snipers. The company made it to the centre of Geilenkirchen at around 0900 hours, by which time Company A had not even reached the outskirts of the town.

Lieutenant-Colonel Woodyard was up with the leading troops. His main worry was the absence of supporting fire to help his men forward. Interviewed after the battle he explained:

One problem was the lack of artillery fire. After the artillery preparation for the jump off, we received no artillery support because it was considered that our own troops, on the flanks, were too close to the enemy for safety in firing.

There was little contact between the two companies, radio communication was erratic and telephone wires were continually being cut by road traffic in the rear. Woodyard had no idea of how Company A was progressing. He sent several patrols from Company C to contact it and find out what was happening, but no information came back. The advance of the right flank had been so rapid that, around 1200 hours, when Company A had eventually reached the centre of the town, Company B was about 1,000 yards in front of it.

The leading company had been advancing up the line of the railway track. Shortly before 1400 hours, it met its first real resistance. Heavy mortar fire fell on the leading troops as they passed over the Suggerath-Geilenkirchen road crossing, some 600 yards north east of the town.

The mortar fire was taken up by some snipers in a house on the hill away to the right, forcing the advancing infantry off the railway and down to the low ground either side of the tracks. The company spread out but did not stop moving. Woodyard urged the riflemen on. As long as its advance was comparatively easy, the company would press on with the attack.

An hour later it arrived as far as the southern edge of Suggerath. Here, resistance stiffened considerably. The leading platoon pushed across the road and was caught in some cross-fire, suffering heavy casualties in the process. 'I held up here for a time to see if it could take care of the German opposition itself,' Lieutenant-Colonel Woodyard recalled 'but it soon became evident that the company would need some help.'

By 1530, the company was so disorganised and scattered that it had become ineffective. Company B had been at point, leading the 1st Battalion, since 0700 hours that morning. It was time for it to take a rest. Woodyard decided that his third company should take over the lead:

I called Lieutenant Stacy, of the British AVRE [Armoured Vehicle Royal Engineers] tanks and Captain Roy Sweitzer, Commander Company C, over and gave them instructions. At this time, the bulk of the tanks were still in Geilenkirchen. There were no good routes of approach open to Suggerath. I instructed Captain Sweitzer to move up the road and pass through Company B. The British tanks were to swing around the right of the railroad, utilising the high ground to support the advance by fire, until such time as they could move onto the Geilenkirchen-Suggerath road and thereafter, to move with the infantry into the village.

In addition to the tanks from the Sherwood Rangers Yeomanry, Woodyard was hoping to use some specialised armour from the British 79th Armoured Division. A squadron of Crocodile flame-throwing tanks from the 141st Regiment Royal Armoured Corps, and a squadron of AVREs from the 42nd Assault Regiment Royal Engineers, had been attached to the American Division. For the attack on Suggerath, Woodyard was given one troop of crocodiles, one troop of AVREs and two troops of the Sherwood Rangers.

The AVRE tank was an assault vehicle based on the British Churchill tank chassis. Its main armament was a spigot mortar, called a Petard, of 29cm calibre and capable of firing a forty pound bomb eighty yards. It was designed specifically to attack fixed defences such as pillboxes. However, the short range of the mortar meant that it had to get close to the emplacement and so the AVRE needed infantry support when making an attack, but it did enable a tremendous punch to be carried right up to the concrete emplacements.

The attack on Suggerath by Company C with the British tanks was launched at 1545 hours. The tank/infantry co-ordination was good. The assault force quickly closed on the village and the riflemen reached the first of the buildings. Resistance was heavy. Sniper and machine gun fire came at the 'Railsplitters' from every direction. The company had orders not to stop there, but to push through the village as fast as they could. The infantry moved along the main road close behind the tanks, seeking shelter from the enemy fire in the lee of the armoured vehicles. Those infantry who followed up were caught in the cross-fire of the Germans who were left inside the buildings. Progress was slow, and the north eastern outskirts of Suggerath were not reached until about 1700 hours. Colonel Woodyard was at the southern end of the village:

> The town obviously hadn't been cleared by our infantry, and I went in to see what the trouble was. Our communications were still out. Reaching the village, I discovered that the infantry was allowing cross-fire and snipers to hold them up. I started them going again.

Company B had been reorganised and followed the commander into Suggerath. Company C had moved back astride the railway line and had stopped. The infantrymen were being shot in the back by the Germans holed up in the village. Woodyard urged the men on. They were not able to do much more, because the light was beginning to fail. Woodyard still wanted his men up on the high ground beyond Suggerath that night. He decided that he would get on up there himself and have a look:

> I felt that if we didn't get organised for the night, we'd get hit. I took six men and worked along the railroad bank. I had a radio operator, four riflemen from Company C and my bodyguard. One of the Company C men got lost and I was reduced to five. We eased our way forward to a point about 600 yards north-east of Suggerath and were just getting ready to go up the high ground on our right, when we became entangled in some telephone wire that the Germans had cut from the telegraph poles alongside the tracks. Then we were ambushed.

Six or seven Germans, spread out on both sides of the railway lines, opened fire. Woodyard and his men dived to the ground, seeking cover. Ahead of them on the railway tracks, a German jumped to his feet and opened up with a machine pistol, firing along the line of the advancing Americans. The man immediately behind the colonel was hit in the throat. The patrol returned the fire and hit two of the enemy.

This counter fire seemed to quieten the enemy troops down. Woodyard thought that they were pulling back and began taking care of the wounded man.

> I got my compress out and put my left arm around him to balance him while I attempted to bandage his wound. He was bleeding fast. Then some Jerry threw a grenade and I was hit in the left arm. I don't know how I wasn't killed. Blood was spurting from my arm.

Woodyard rolled over, still tangled up in the wire. He could not see a thing in the darkness and did not know if the wounded man he was holding was dead or not. Berkowski, his bodyguard, told him that two of the others were dead. The colonel knew that they could not go any further along the railway line. They were already on the best ground. He decided that the patrol would have to crawl back to Company C's positions for help to get the wounded out. By this time it was around 1830 hours and quite dark.

Earlier that afternoon, at 1430 hours, Company A set out from Geilenkirchen in a single column and wound its way out of the town in the direction of Trips, a small hamlet on the road to Randerath. The movement was unopposed and uneventful until they had quit the built-up area and moved out onto the open road. Then the company started to receive automatic weapons and mortar fire, backed up by artillery, which sent the troops scurrying for cover into a nearby grove of trees. Mortar rounds and shells exploded in the trees above the troops, showering the area with splinters of steel.

The fire appeared to be coming from a steep hill, to the left of the road, in the British sector. The suspected enemy position completely overlooked the road and afforded them excellent observation of the route out of Geilenkirchen. Tanks of the Sherwood Rangers were brought up to shell the area. As John J. O'Malley watched a tank crew firing their cannon at the hill, it reminded him of a training exercise – it was so smoothly carried out.

Just beyond that hill were the British lines. Men of the 5th Duke of Cornwall's Light Infantry were dug in on the adjacent piece of high ground. The Cornwalls had spent that morning cleaning weapons and resting as much as possible while D Company waited for the Americans to press home their attack on Geilenkirchen. In the early afternoon, things began to happen. First, a few German troops were seen approaching D Company's positions from the direction of the town. Then, gradually, the numbers began to increase and it soon became apparent that about forty of them had worked their way into the wood and were trying to break through the Cornwalls' defences. All three of the company's forward platoons soon felt the full force of the attack.

It was now obvious to the men of the 5th DCLI that the enemy in Geilenkirchen were trying to carve themselves out an escape route from the town. Three German self-propelled guns joined in the melee and the onslaught developed into a full-scale assault. Every conceivable weapon seemed to be firing at the Wessexmen. D Company's situation became increasingly worrying when an enemy tank penetrated the centre of its positions and neutralised an anti-tank crew. Colonel Taylor made ready C Company to go to D Company's aid. Then the Americans put in an appearance.

By this time, it was late afternoon. The shadows were lengthening when Company A of the 1st Battalion, the 333rd Regiment, was told that they would have to take that hill by nightfall. The men were roused out of their shallow foxholes and moved up the road until they were opposite the village of Suggerath on the other side of the River Wurm. Then they waited and watched as the Sherwood Rangers blasted the hilltop with cannon and machine gun fire. When the firing lifted, the Americans dashed across the road and climbed the steep slope by pulling themselves up from one bush or tree to the next. On the top, they found an open field bounded on three sides by trees. There had been no resistance; the Germans defending the hill had fled. The enemy had no desire to get trapped between the attacking American infantry and the dug in defensive positions of the British. The area fell quiet as Company A prepared to dig in for the night.

Lieutenant-Colonel Woodyard had halted his battalion and consolidated his positions. Company C had sent a platoon forward and wiped out the resistance on the high ground, while the remainder of the company were digging in and organising the defence of Suggerath. The village behind them was still not clear of the enemy, and sniper fire was continually harassing their rear. Assistance was on the way from the regiment's 3rd Battalion to help clear all the captured ground that had been by-passed by the attacking troops, but the enemy was everywhere. Nobody was safe travelling along the roads out of Geilenkirchen.

Woodyard was suffering from his wound. He insisted that he remain with his men until the reinforcements from the 3rd Battalion arrived. At 2330 hours, after two companies had moved into Suggerath, he succumbed: 'I was getting pretty damned weak from loss of blood. I was shaking all over and it was damned cold. They evacuated me then.'

Situation at 2330 hours, Sunday, 19 November
The main objective of XXX Corps' Operation Clipper had been taken: the US 84th Division had captured Geilenkirchen. The 333rd Regiment had two battalions in the Wurm Valley, had taken Suggerath and had met up with the British 43rd Division. The German salient had been removed, but the battle was not yet over.

It was now important that the recent gains should be consolidated and enlarged, so as to keep pace with the other American attacks by the 2nd Armored and 102nd Infantry Divisions on the right. It was XXX Corps' responsibility to protect their northern flank as they fought their way towards the River Roer. To do this, Horrocks ordered that all units would resume the attack the next day.

Chapter Eleven

The Second Night

Brigadier-General Bolling was pleased with his division's performance that day: 'The 84th has displayed the finest qualities for a new division under direct fire that I have ever seen. They are acting like veterans.' That evening, the general received a visitor at his headquarters.

The Corps Commander had come over to congratulate Bolling on the day's events. Horrocks was full of praise for the way the division had handled the capture of Geilenkirchen and the enemy resistance, but he added a word of caution. He warned that worse was to come. Horrocks knew from bitter experience that the enemy usually kept some of its best men in reserve to try immediately to recapture its losses. He told Bolling to expect first class troops from the 15th Panzer Grenadier and the 9th Panzer Division to come at him either that night or in the morning.

To the average infantryman, the questions of strategy and tactics discussed by generals were a complete mystery. Gil Bradham was a private in Company C of the 333rd Regiment:

> I don't remember ever being briefed as to what our objective was to be, only that we were to move into some designated position, or to hold a position, or to move to some new position for a possible counter attack. We did not spend long in Geilenkirchen, our job was mopping up the few snipers that were left in the town. We then seemed to be moved about a lot, walking mostly, sometimes digging in at two or three locations that night. After having moved at least twice, I was so tired that I just wrapped myself in my raincoat, lay down and went to sleep. There was a little rain during the night and the next morning I awoke soaked to the skin. All I could find to drink was cold black coffee.

Company C was dug in just outside the northern edge of Suggerath. In the village behind them, some of the buildings still contained German soldiers. The houses were proving to be very difficult to clear, especially those that backed on to the meadows near the river. The river valley was still wide open to the enemy. The 1st Battalion of the 333rd Regiment did not have enough troops on the ground to completely hold the area. Companies B and C were in and around Suggerath, while D was behind in reserve. Some of the 3rd Battalion had come up to the village but had not moved out into the marshy ground near the river. Company A was on the other side of the river, holding the hill overlooking the main road out of Geilenkirchen.

If the enemy troops in Suggerath could not be flushed out by small arms fire, then they would have to be burned out. Two British Crocodile tanks were brought up to set fire to the houses. The great lumbering saurians moved through the village from house to house, shooting long flaming arcs of burning napalm into the buildings. Those of the enemy who did not surrender or run were burned alive.

On the other side of the river to the north-west of the road out of Geilenkirchen, Company A covered the American extreme left flank. Strictly speaking, it was on British territory, for the Geilenkirchen-Randerath road was the boundary between the US 84th and the Wessex Division, and Company A were on the hill to the left of this road. John J. O'Malley had dug in for the night:

> The foxhole that Junior and I shared was next to the woods at the edge of the hill facing Geilenkirchen. After we had organised our defence for the night, we stood in the trench watching some British Churchill flamethrowing tanks move slowly through Suggerath burning one building after another. As night fell, the flames reflecting off of the clouds created a scene reminiscent of Dante's *Inferno*. All through the night the village quietly burned, an unforgettable sight. Even though one of us should have stayed awake during the night, the exertions of our first day in action were simply too much and we both eventually fell asleep, exhausted.

The company was rudely awakened in the middle of the night by bright yellow tracer bullets passing low over its position. O'Malley was certain that the Germans had zeroed in on his particular foxhole and that the company was being counter attacked. His great fear was that he and Junior would be plucked out of their hole without a fight. The thought of being captured by the enemy was a fate too ignominious to contemplate. He grabbed his rifle and made ready for the expected onslaught. It never came. The enemy fire had been aimed at the British and had come from the direction of Tripsrath.

The remainder of the night was pitch black, apart from the faint light cast by the burning village. No movement was seen on the hill. O'Malley had no trouble in staying awake and alert during the rest of the night.

The 3rd Battalion of the 333rd Regiment had cleared most of Geilenkirchen of the enemy during the latter part of the day. Corporal Richard Roush was a stretcher bearer with the battalion and had stood by the side of the road watching the men move up into the town, waiting to fall in behind them at the end of the column. He remembers one particular man smiling as he passed him calling out, 'Doc, I'm going up there and getting me a mess of them Krauts.' Roush laughed and shouted back, 'You just watch them, they may get a mess of you!' Roush was impressed with the young man's confidence and enthusiasm. After all the months of training, he seemed to be anxious to get at the enemy, but then again perhaps it was just an outburst of nervous energy. Roush found him shot dead a few days later.

Company K had swept through the town clearing each house in turn and taking almost a hundred enemy soldiers prisoner in the process. All were from the 183rd Volks Grenadier Division. Most of them were old men or young boys. They had hidden in the cellars when the artillery preparation for the 1st Battalion's attack had come in that morning, and had stayed put for the rest of the day, waiting for a suitable chance to surrender. Company K then moved out of the town along the road to the north and dug in between the river and Company A.

The 3rd Battalion's other companies all passed through Geilenkirchen and dug in to the north-east of the town. Patrols were sent out that night to gather information and contact the other units on either side of them. They found that the whole area ahead of the battalion was thick with German troops. One successful patrol from Company K managed to get as far down the valley as Wurm, but was captured near the village.

Some of the enemy were not in the town when it was captured yet still wished to surrender. Quite often they took cover and waited for the fighting to pass on by before they considered it safe enough to show themselves. Roy Long, a private with the 309th Engineer Battalion remembers one such group of Germans:

> I was changing a tyre on my jeep that had been hit by shrapnel, when I heard a noise behind me. I turned and found a party of about eighteen to twenty enemy soldiers standing beside me with their hands on their heads. My gun was in the jeep on the back seat. I made a quick grab for it, but only succeeded in picking up a flare pistol that was laying alongside. It was still enough to do the trick, for the group of Germans obeyed my every move as I escorted them back to the rear and into the arms of some MPs that I met on the road.

Since 0900 hours that morning, the US 405th Infantry Regiment had been attached to the 84th Division. Although the regiment had been under Bolling's control since 17 November, he had been told by the Ninth Army's Commander, General William Simpson, that it could be committed 'only in case of emergency.'

Earlier that morning it seemed to Bolling that he had an emergency on his hands when he considered that his right flank was 'sort of out in the breeze,' and had moved the 2nd Battalion of the 405th Regiment into a position to the left of Immendorf in case of counter attack. Now that Geilenkirchen had been captured, he decided to use another battalion of the 405th, the 3rd Battalion, to finish clearing the town and then hold it while his 333rd Regiment moved on down the Wurm Valley.

The 405th's 3rd Battalion moved into Geilenkirchen as the 333rd Regiment's 3rd Battalion moved out. Once the town had been cleared finally of all enemy snipers and hidden German soldiers, the men of the 405th could relax a little. By that time, each man considered himself to be a combat veteran, which meant they had no more fears of incoming shells in the daytime and could set about a systematic exploration of the town.

Bob Enkelmann discovered a part demolished 'apotheke', which he assured his fellow squad members was a drugstore. Exhaustive excavation of the remains of the store resulted in the discovery of a stock of bubble bath. This was a prize find and led to 'one of the biggest cleanliness campaigns of the war,' as Enkelmann himself explains:

> In our air-conditioned squad CP, a bathroom was found on the second floor. Although the roof of the house was gone, and artillery shells were known to whistle overhead into the next yard, these things did not deter our squad members from cleaning out the debris from the bathroom and the tub. Then it was a simple matter of convincing the cooks to reheat the barrels of water used to clean the mess tins, to provide water for a company bath. Little incentive was needed to get the men into the tub; the liberal use of the scented bubble bath and the thought of soaking until you smelled as though you had just emerged from a Parisian house of ill repute, were temptations enough. It was a pleasant thought to know that you could have your arse blown to kingdom come, but still arrive at the Pearly Gates smelling like an angel.

Benjamin Gerber from the anti-tank company was on guard duty that night in Geilenkirchen. Gerber and his buddy Ray Weinstein were covering a road into the town. Two men approached them in the dark. They halted when requested, but did not know the password. It was pitch dark and neither of the 'Ozarks' could see a thing, so they ordered the two strangers to drop their weapons and come slowly forward with their hands up. Gerber recalls what happened next:

We questioned them closely but they did not know who their commanding officer was, or the names of their platoon or squad leader. We decided to take them prisoner until the next morning when we could better deal with them. We tied them up hand and foot with number ten telephone wire and put them in the corner of a room. The next morning we discovered, just by looking at them, that they were Mexican–Americans. It turned out that the reason they did not know anything about their unit was because they were new replacements who had gotten lost and were terrified to death of us!

Over on the 334th Regiment's side of the battlefield, the night was fairly quiet. Prummern was clear of Germans, but many others were still close by on Mahogany Hill. All three battalions had established positions in foxholes around the village, covering the forward edge in a great arc.

Further out to the right, the 2nd Armored Division had progressed a little further towards Gereonsweiler and the 102nd Infantry were filling in the gap between it and the 84th. The 405th Infantry Regiment held the rear.

For the Wessex Division, the night was long, cold, wet and uncomfortable. All of their positions were under shell fire from the guns on the hills to the east of the river. While the Americans were inside the Siegfried Line amongst the fortifications, the British were outside, 'beneath the walls'. The Germans completely overlooked the 43rd Division's sector and had every point registered.

The 1st Worcestershires in Tripsrath seemed to suffer some of the worst of the shelling. The enemy knew that this village formed the northern anchor of the XXX Corps' hold on the area, and were determined to make it uninhabitable, prior to its recapture. Tripsrath was subjected to almost constant bombardment. The regimental history states:

> The German guns were numerous, of large calibre, and apparently well supplied with ammunition. In addition, the gunners knew their business and their ranges, and the battalion knew again the exasperation of sitting in a slit trench, or in a cellar, and being hit and hit without opportunity of hitting back.

Casualties are never very high if those on the receiving end are below ground in trenches or cellars. The main effect is nervous strain and the lowering of the morale of the men under fire.

In one of the slit trenches in Tripsrath that night was Private Eric Tipping:

> We had by that time learned how near a shell would fall, by the sound it made in flight. Being below ground reduced casualties, but to be in a

shallow slit trench under prolonged shell and mortar fire can push a man to the limits. I found it made me dig deep into my inner self to stop the panic; it forced me ask myself how much more could I take before I cracked. As the shells fell nearer and nearer to my trench, the noise made my head feel as though it was going to split open. I had to fight myself from giving in to the strain and getting up and running away from it all; I knew it had to be endured. I recall forcing myself to think of other things in my life that I had known before all this. As the shells moved away, being young, I was able to quickly compose myself back to near normal. I say near normal, because I must admit that ever afterwards I had a dread of being caught above ground during an artillery barrage. Such was the strain at the time, that I remember cursing when one of our tanks started up its engine as I knew that the noise would bring more shells down on us. When you looked at the size of the craters and the closeness to which they had fallen to our slits, it was amazing that any of us still remained alive. But like all things in life, there is an element of luck, or fate, or help from above, depending on your viewpoint.

In the woods either side of Tripsrath, it was the same story, although the shell fire there brought added hazards. Being surrounded by dense forest brought no real cover. The tall trees exploded the incoming shells in the air above the slit trenches, showering the area beneath with shrapnel. Crashing trees and falling branches added to the danger. The Wessexmen could only cower in their shallow trenches while red hot pieces of steel rained vertically down on them. It brought each man close to the bounds of his endurance.

There is never any perfect ground on which to fight. If the terrain were open, such as that which confronted the 334th Regiment, all movement could be seen. Without cover to move behind during an attack, the infantryman is naked. The opposite is also true when in defence; too much cover allows the enemy to approach unseen. He can infiltrate positions to get behind the lines and cause havoc in the rear. That night, in the dark woods of Germany, the enemy seemed to be everywhere. Sniper and mortar fire now came at the Wessexmen from all directions, adding to their discomfort.

The 5th Dorsets and the 7th Somersets had only paused for the night. They were both expected to advance the next morning to capture the remainder of their respective woods. After almost two days of continuous action there was still very little opportunity for sleep. Preparations had to be made for the morning's advance. Supplies had to be got up to them along the muddy tracks through the woods, although this proved to be nigh impossible. By the time the first light filtered through the rain sodden branches, the men were all but exhausted. It took a supreme effort for them to haul their cold, wet bodies out of the waterlogged foxholes and set themselves to face the horror of yet another advance. For the third day running, they were on the offensive.

Between the 7th Somerset Light Infantry and the Americans was the 5th Duke of Cornwall's Light Infantry. Its Commander, Lieutenant-Colonel George Taylor was not displeased with the initial phase of the battle:

> The American assault down the Wurm Valley had met with fierce resistance after its initial success. Blazing British tanks of the Sherwood Rangers could be seen from our positions. We had lost one of our fine young officers through a direct hit on his slit trench during the intense shelling of our positions on the southern edge of Hocheid Wood. I took immediate steps to reduce the number of platoons in the wood. Otherwise, the 5th DCLI had got off rather lightly in the battle to support the taking of Geilenkirchen. Our casualty list was one dead and four wounded. We had inflicted at least twenty-one dead and nine wounded on the Germans. In addition, we had knocked out three self-propelled guns and taken many prisoners.

Generalleutnant Wolfgang Lange had realised long before the American attack had begun that Geilenkirchen could not be held by his 183rd Volks Grenadier Division. The 1st Battalion of the 343rd Regiment was in no fit state to repel an assault by a fresh American division. Lange requested that the town be surrendered and his men withdrawn to a new defensive line at Mullendorf. Authority for this move was not granted until the encirclement was complete and the technical means of communication were gone. Patrols that were to deliver the order to pull out either could not find their way, or could not find their own troops. As a result, an entire German battalion was lost in Geilenkirchen, yet nothing essential had been gained.

A counter attack was ordered, 'Perhaps solely out of habit,' wrote Lange after the war.

> The 104th Panzer Grenadier Regiment, of the 15th Panzer Grenadiers, was brought into the Tripsrath area and assigned to the division. It was ordered to retake Geilenkirchen with an attack to the south. Although the direction of attack and the terrain were favourable, the attack had little prospects of success from the outset because the German forces operating there were too weak. They were halted in the Niederheide area after some initial success. However, the higher command was satisfied.

This was the enemy attack that had been stopped by the 1st Worcestershires earlier that day. These 104th Panzer Grenadiers were now in the woods in front of the 5th Dorsets.

Lange was critical of his higher command. He was concerned as to whether the higher command actually had misjudged the situation, or whether it knew from the outset that the counter attack was doomed to failure. 'Perhaps the higher command only intended to narrow the penetration or seal it off,' he wrote. 'If this were true, the orders were both tactically wrong and immoral.'

In any event, the 183rd Division was only a delaying force. The design of the Westwall had always planned for this. Once the fortifications had been penetrated, the mobile panzers behind them would take over and pinch out the attackers. The 9th Panzer and 15th Panzer Grenadier Divisions were now waiting to do just that.

After this initial phase of the battle, some American reinforcements were sent up to the front to replenish the troop losses of the first two days. Joe Curtis was a replacement infantryman for Company C, 1st Battalion, 334th Regiment. He well remembers his move up to the line:

> We had just passed an enclosed courtyard and had to stop for a few minutes to let some trucks come into the road and head back for Palenberg, which we had just left. One of the trucks stopped as it turned in front of me, so I managed to look inside the rear to see what they were hauling. All I could see were bodies piled up, with arms and legs askew. They had used this courtyard to gather up the dead from the battlefield, both American and German, and then haul them to the rear to be separated and buried. The sight was shocking to me. I now knew that I was in a combat zone for sure, with a real possibility of being killed or wounded.

It was a sobering experience for any man to be confronted by the bodies of his dead comrades when going into action. The sight reminded him too much of his own frail mortality. Nonetheless, as with every battle, there were the dead to contend with. Frank Kuplin was unfortunate enough to be picked for one of the worst jobs:

> We were sent out on a detail to pick up bodies of both sides and haul them back to a graves registration unit. As we went back through the town, the people would turn their backs on the sight.

Americans were not to be buried in Germany, but taken right back by special mobile collecting units to military cemeteries being established in Holland. From the British point of view, this approach destroyed something that was very precious to their traditions, as the Reverend Leslie Skinner, Chaplain of the Sherwood Rangers Yeomanry, recalls:

> It was our custom to bury the dead near to where they fell, and at some considerably later date, perhaps even after the end of the war, Grave

Registration Units would exhume the bodies and re-bury them in permanent War Graves Cemeteries. It was my job to make sure I collected our own casualties, buried them, marked the graves and then, as soon as may be, write to the family of each man killed giving brief details, words of comfort and some account of where and how their boy had been buried.

One of the places that Reverend Skinner selected for the burial of some of the Sherwood Rangers' casualties was a few yards off the road near a crossroads outside Apweiler, on the road to Geilenkirchen. The spot was just about half a mile from where the fighting was still going on. He dug eight graves, buried the men and was just finishing marking the crosses, when a British flail tank pulled off the road a few yards from him. An American half-track did the same a few yards further on. As the tank backed into position, it ran over a mine. The explosion killed the co-driver and wounded four of the Americans dismounting from their half-track. Reverend Skinner was unhurt. 'It was only when we had dealt with the casualties that it dawned on me that I had dug eight graves in a mine field,' he recalled. 'One felt that the American system had more to commend it than I had thought!'

In contrast to the caring attitude of the clergy, there was the other side of war, the grisly, brutalising side. James Meehan talks of the GI who used to drag several still warm bodies together and sleep on them to keep from lying on the wet ground. Another story was of the telegraph operator who set up his post in the bombed-out remains of a basement. The graves registration group had been busy picking up bits and pieces of casualties and stacking the sacks against the outside wall. Stray cats kept dragging part of these remains back and forth during the night, until it drove the operator berserk.

Situation at 0600 hours, Monday, 20 November
There had been no enemy counter attacks against the gains made by XXX Corps. The night had been a time for consolidation. The Americans were in firm control of Geilenkirchen and Prummern, but knew the enemy were only yards in front of them blocking the way forward. The British front line was less well defined. It straggled its way through two dense woods and a village that was shared with the enemy. The new day would see how well the enemy might exploit the situation.

Chapter Twelve

Monday, 20 November

On the morning of 20 November, the battle for the Geilenkirchen salient was almost two days old. Both sides now sized up the situation. To the enemy High Command, XXX Corps' attack was just one of many he was suffering all along the Westwall. Operation Clipper was not seen by him in isolation. It was just part of the general offensive that was taking place in the area between the Wurm and Roer rivers. The German XII SS Corps, defending the area between Baesweiler and Maeseyck, was also dealing with the attacks being made by the US XIX Corps, as the 2nd Armored and 102nd Divisions advanced towards Gereonsweiler.

The German XII SS Corps, commanded by General der Infantrie Günther Blumentritt, consisted of just the 176th and 183rd Infantry Divisions and was in place to hold the main line of defence. Behind them, in reserve when the American attack began, was the German XLVII Panzer Corps, commanded by General Heinrich Von Luettwitz. The Corps comprised of the 9th Panzer and the 15th Panzer Grenadier Divisions.

The fighting in and around Geilenkirchen had taken its toll of the troops of General Lange's 183rd Volks Grenadier Division. Much depleted, the division was placed under the control of XLVII Corps. Five of the division's battalions were completely exhausted or reduced to a small cadre. Only the 351st Grenadier Regiment, commanded by Colonel Schudo, on the division's left wing had escaped the worst of the fighting. Consequently, Lange's headquarters was temporarily withdrawn from the front to reorganise the five battalions and the engineering battalion. The 351st Regiment and the division's artillery regiment was divided between the 9th Panzer and 15th Panzer Grenadier Divisions.

This reserve force of the XLVII had been committed in part on 16 November, when the 9th Panzer Division counter attacked the US 2nd Armored at Immendorf. Since that time, it had been introduced into the action piecemeal to stop up holes that had appeared in the line. The same was true for the 15th Panzer Grenadiers.

The 15th Panzer Grenadiers had recently arrived back in Germany from Italy. The men of the division had a nickname for their unit: 'Zitter Division' (Shiver Division). The majority of the personnel of the division were feeling the cold because they were still wearing the light uniform issued to them in the Italian Campaign. General Rodt, their commander at the time of the move, had requested warm clothing for his men at frequent intervals, but he had been told that all uniforms were needed for the new volks grenadier divisions. At the time of the Geilenkirchen battle, Rodt had been temporarily replaced by Colonel Simeon, and there was news that he too was soon to be superseded by an SS general, much to the chagrin of the regular army officers.

Elements of the division had also joined the 9th Panzers in the counter attacks against the US XIX Corps between Immendorf and Gereonsweiler. However, on 19 November, other units of the 15th Panzer Grenadiers, notably from the 104th Regiment, had been in action on the other side of the battlefield against the British in Tripsrath. They were also found to be blocking the 333rd Regiment's way down the Wurm Valley that same evening. All this indicated that the resistance in front of XXX Corps had been reinforced by first class troops. The Corps was no longer attacking positions held by poorly trained volks grenadiers, but by the tanks and infantry of the panzer divisions.

Lieutenant-General Horrocks looked at his map and saw that his front line had become a little ragged. It needed straightening out. He decided that the day would be spent tidying up the battlefield and bringing the Corps into line.

On the left, the British would take the two woods either side of Tripsrath and produce a wide arc that would protect the 333rd Regiment's left flank as it advanced up the Wurm Valley. In the centre, the 333rd would clear out Suggerath, establish the 1st Battalion in a strong position across the valley and then send the 3rd Battalion against the villages of Mullendorf and Wurm. Its 2nd Battalion would stay in reserve, ready to exploit any gains made by the attack. On the right, the 334th Regiment would take Mahogany Hill and then advance on Beeck, to keep abreast of the 2nd Armored Division on its right.

The 5th Dorsets had spent the night in the woods under almost continual shell and mortar fire. By morning, the men were tired, cold and hungry. The troops were entering their third day of battle. Lieutenant-Colonel Venour had evolved a new plan for the resumption of the attack through the wood. D Company was to lead the battalion across the exposed gap and move straight ahead towards the northern end of the wood. B Company, following slightly behind and to the left, intended to move up along the western edge. Next would come the remainder of the battalion. Owing to the heavy casualties suffered the day before, A and C Companies were amalgamated into one company, under the command of Major

Harry Allen. Their objective was the right hand, northern corner of the wood alongside Tripsrath.

What made this attack different from the previous attempt the day before was the weight of fire that was to be put at the Dorsets' disposal to support the move. The whole of the division's artillery was ready to shoot them in. Field guns, medium guns and 3-inch mortars would start the action at 0830 hours, with a ten-minute barrage on the forward edge of the wood on the other side of the gap. The bombardment would then lift and the guns would continue to put down a series of concentrations further and further into the wood. The Dorsets could advance across the gap behind the comparative safety of this rolling barrage. In addition, two troops of tanks from the 13th/18th Royal Hussars were to move around either flank and rake the forest with their Besa machine guns and main armament. Overwhelming firepower was to be the bludgeon to get the battalion onto its objective.

At 0830 hours to the second, the attack began. Twenty minutes later, the companies were across the open ground and into the northern section of woods. Initially, except for some artillery and mortar fire, they had met no opposition. The enemy infantry had withdrawn into the forest. However, after an advance of about two hundred yards, D Company found them again. Mortar and small arms fire came out of the trees at the advancing troops. German resistance had been resumed. D Company fought every inch of the way to its objective. By 0950 hours, Major Hartwell's company had made it. The Dorsets were now on the northern edge of the wood looking out across open country towards Straeten and Waldenrath. Within another hour, so were the remainder of the battalion. Of the 104 enemy prisoners who had been taken, most were wounded. By 1100 hours, all the battalion's objectives had been occupied.

The 5th Dorsets now had the complete wood, but it had little strength other than manpower to hold it. None of the tanks had made it up with the leading companies through the mud, nor could any anti-tank guns get forward to them. The main axis for the supporting arms up to the new front line was overlooked by the enemy. Each man or machine going forward came under German observation.

Now the problems began. The troops of the 15th Panzer Grenadiers had given up the wood, but they soon wanted it back again. The 104th Panzer Regiment could see all that the men of the 5th Dorsets were doing from its positions in Straeten. The northern end of the forest was just a couple of hundred yards away. Under perfect observation, the enemy now brought down a tremendous barrage on the Dorsets' new positions. Most of the Wessexmen were caught unprotected trying to dig themselves slit trenches. The casualties quickly began to mount. Then two German self-propelled guns moved up to the edge of Straeten and began to pump shells into the area from close range over open sights. Twice the panzer grenadiers tried to form up in the village for a counter attack, but each time they did they were dispersed by the 43rd Division's artillery.

In the midst of the chaos and fire that was falling all around the 5th Dorsets, the Royal Artillery had forward observation officers up with the leading troops to control the guns in the rear. The 112th Field Artillery was supporting the battalion, and Bombardier Ron Barber was the carrier driver for his troop's commander, Captain Jack Gilders. The pair of them were on foot and came under some heavy mortar fire as they tried to find B Company's headquarters in the woods.

Gilders told the bombardier to go back and bring up their carrier which was parked about one hundred yards behind. When Barber returned, he found that his captain had been hit in the back by shrapnel.

I put him in the back of the carrier as carefully as possible and tried to get him back to the aid station, but the going was bad. We found our Battery Commander, Major Loosley, at the Dorsets' battalion HQ and he came out to speak to Captain Gilders. Despite his wounds, the captain was able to give the bearings of the very mortars that had got him. Because the thick mud was causing chaos with all the transport, I was told to take the wounded captain all the way back to the aid post. The going was very difficult. Heavy mud clogged the tracks of our carrier and sent us spinning round in circles on the spot. We found an aid post but there was little they could do for him and I was told to take him further back to a field surgical unit. When we arrived there I said goodbye to Captain Gilders. He died the next day. The whole troop was very upset. He was an extremely popular man; we used to call him Captain Jack.

There were many such casualties in the woods that day. The shelling was some of the worst the battalion had ever suffered. Conditions were dreadful. Major Hartwell was completely buried when a large calibre shell landed alongside his trench. He was dug out alive, but only just in time. Dogged resistance kept the 5th Dorsets in their positions. The battalion hung on tenaciously to its gains. 'It had fought many hard battles,' wrote Brigadier Essame, 'but few harder than this or at a higher price. Altogether, an entire battalion of first class German troops had been destroyed by the Dorsets.'

It was time to pull the battalion out of the woods. Arrangements were made for its sister battalion, the 4th Dorsets, to relieve it later that night. As a tribute to the magnificent fighting carried out by the battalion during the two days, the Divisional Commander decreed that the woods should be henceforth known as 'Dorset Wood'. The action had cost the battalion seventy men, killed, wounded or missing.

In the woods between Hocheid and Hoven, the 7th Somerset Light Infantry experienced much the same problems as the 5th Dorsets had done. Muddy, cold, wet, hungry and worn out by shell fire, the men had a miserable existence. There was only one route up to the forward companies and this led outside the woods, facing the open fields to the north. The track was thick with mud and sloped alarmingly towards the drainage ditches that ran alongside. To make matters worse, it was in full view of the enemy. Many vehicles came to grief along this route forward, one of the first being Lieutenant-Colonel Borradaile's carrier as he travelled up to inspect his forward positions.

During the night, attempts were made to get anti-tank guns and food up to the troops dug just back from the edge of the gap in the middle of the woods. Either the ditch, or the enemy, claimed them all. By morning, eight vehicles and a horse-drawn cart were bogged down alongside the track. Nothing, other than the men themselves, managed to get forward throughout the day or the night.

Sergeant Dan Robertson was having an uncomfortable time in the forest.

Day break and 'stand to'. No food had been brought up to us during the previous night, we had survived on our compo rations. There had been no enemy counter attack, just endless mortar and artillery fire. The weather was foul. The wood, which was untouched when our attack started, was now taking on the aspect of a World War I battlefield. All the trees were blasted and broken.

The 7th Somersets were in a hopeless position. Virtually every movement had come to a halt. The enemy were on the other side of the narrow gap in the forest, causing a great deal of interference. The men of the 15th Panzer Grenadiers were at home in the woods and used the thick cover to their advantage. They would creep surreptitiously through the undergrowth and snipe at the Somersets from the rear. Every tree seemed to conceal one of the enemy.

The day's attack against the northern part of the wood never got started. The mud and the disorganised state of the battalion, forced the move to be cancelled. The most important objective for the 7th Somersets that day was merely to survive in its present position.

The average monthly rainfall for the Geilenkirchen area of Germany in November is 2.25 inches. In 1944, almost double that amount of rain fell. In a normal year, rain could be expected on an average of fifteen days during the month of November. In 1944, rain was recorded on twenty-eight days.

The skies above Geilenkirchen that winter were perpetually cloudy. The rain that fell turned the earth into a soggy sponge. Little of the water had a chance to evaporate under the overcast skies. The result was an endless bog of waterlogged fields and woods. Any unmetalled roads quickly disintegrated into rutted paths of mud. Vehicular movement off the roads was virtually impossible. Caterpillar tracks helped, but even tanks found it hard going – except, that is, for the enemy's whose armoured vehicles were equipped with wider tracks and seemed to be able to glide across the glutinous mud.

The overcast skies also forced air support to be curtailed or postponed, thus eliminating one very special advantage that the Allies had over their enemy. At that time in the war, the Allied air forces had complete mastery of the air. Every night, heavy bombers pounded German manufacturing industries. Every day, fighter-bombers roamed the skies behind the German front lines, ready to pounce on any significant enemy formations. They interrupted rail and road traffic for hundreds of miles in the rear. They were also very useful in the support of ground troops, able to dive on individual tanks or strongpoints and eliminate them with bombs and rockets.

Both British and American armies had the support of their own tactical air force groups. At Geilenkirchen, the British No 83 Group, Second Tactical Air Force, Royal Air Force was in action. During 19 and 20 November, it managed a few missions with Typhoon rocket-firing aircraft against enemy forces in Wurm and Beeck, but on both days the weather closed in and they had to withdraw to find targets elsewhere in Germany.

Colonel Roosma of the 334th Regiment had to ask his three battalions for another all out effort that morning. It would mean the third day of continuous action for his 1st and 2nd Battalions, but Mahogany Hill and the approach to Beeck had to be taken. The 334th Regiment could not sit in Prummern for ever.

Once more, the 3rd Battalion set out to attack the strongpoint of Mahogany Hill. As a prelude, at 0800 hours, an assault company was sent ahead to take the two pillboxes on the crossroads at the base of it. Thirty minutes later, reports reached the Regimental Command Post that a counter attack by fifteen tanks was coming down the road from the direction of Beeck. Next, there was a frantic message from the assault company that it had been stopped by small arms and 88mm fire.

The 9th Panzer Division, in the shape of the 10th Panzer Regiment, was trying to regain Prummern. The enemy attack was a half-hearted affair, and was broken up by the combined guns of the 334th Regiment and the 84th Division, supported by tanks of the Sherwood Rangers.

During the counter attack, Thomas Kyle and his company became pinned down by some accurate fire from enemy machine guns and artillery unable to move. After a short while a group of the Sherman tanks from the Sherwood Rangers moved up to give support:

One tank stopped right in front of where the first platoon was, in fact it was so close I could have spit on it. The tank immediately started pumping

75mm shells at the Germans. After getting off a few shots, an enemy 88mm shell scored a hit on the tank and tore off the track on the side nearest to me. Even though I was a greenhorn, I knew that the tank's crew should have baled out because the tank was now a sitting duck. But they stayed on and got two more shots off. They took another direct hit, this time right in the middle. Only two Brits came out of the hatches and both of them were wounded. I called for a medic to take care of them. By this time the tank was burning fiercely and we were told to move forward. I will never forget the guts of those tankers.

By 0920 hours, Roosma was able to tell Divisional HQ that there had not been any penetration of his lines and that everything was under control. Anti-tank guns, on the edge of the village, had chased off any of the tanks that had managed to get too close to Prummern.

Panic over, the 3rd Battalion continued its attempts to get at the crossroads beneath its objective. All endeavours came to nothing. The German troops on top of Mahogany Hill looked right down into the streets of Prummern. Their observation was perfect. Each time the 'Railsplitters' moved out to attack, so artillery and mortar fire would drive them back under cover.

The whole day was spent hammering the two pillboxes at the crossroads. Late in the afternoon, just as the light was beginning to fail, much needed support was received by the 3rd Battalion in the shape of two Crocodile flame-throwing tanks. The tanks emerged from the village and drove head on at the pillboxes. About 75 yards from the first bunker, they paused momentarily and emitted long bursts of liquid fire. The flaming jelly splattered against the concrete walls of the pillbox, covering it with a shroud of burning death. Moments later, the second box was hit. Great palls of black smoke drifted skywards. It was an awesome sight as the 'Railsplitters' divisional historian explains:

> The men who were lucky enough to see the spectacle momentarily forgot the mud and the danger of Mahogany Hill. It was one of those terrible and beautiful sights that machines of war create so often almost in spite of themselves, which seem all the more unreal against the ugly reality of war. Once the Crocodiles had worked them over, those pillboxes were black, shrunken coffins. Inside, as soon as the flames had penetrated, the heat became inhuman.

There were no survivors of the attack, no one came out of the concrete tombs. By nightfall, the crossroads had been taken. The Regiment was a few steps closer to the top of Mahogany Hill, but no more secure in its resting place for the night as a result of the gains. The German defenders still looked down on the men dug in around the base.

As for the 334th's 2nd Battalion, it had done little except endure hostile shell fire. Its positions were almost untenable. The high ground between Prummern and Suggerath was a most inhospitable area. The battalion lived in holes in the ground. No progress was made that day on the seemingly endless journey to the village of Beeck that had begun two days previously. It was a hopeless route, the German defenders had the battalion silhouetted against the sky. Men and tanks were obvious targets.

Back in the town of Geilenkirchen, Private First Class Walter E. Ruff of the 405th Regiment's 2nd Battalion Headquarters had a little time on his hands. A previous scouting expedition through the ruins of the town had revealed that just down the street from his CP was the bombed-out remains of what he imagined to be the town's bank. Deep inside the building, in one of the back rooms, was a very important looking unopened safe sitting on a table against the wall.

Ruff was convinced that the safe just had to contain much valuable loot: 'Diamonds, gold, coins and God knows what else,' he thought. He appraised one of his old friends, Lieutenant Dabney C. McCann, of the situation and elicited his help in blowing the safe. Together, they went back to the ammunition dump in the rear and, with the aid of McCann's lieutenant's bar, persuaded the sergeant in charge there to give them six percussion grenades.

Back at the bank, they taped the grenades to the front of the safe across the door. The room containing the safe was reached from the street through a long corridor, with a right-angled bend at each end. Ruff decided that, as he was six feet four inches and weighed 235 pounds, it might be best if the diminutive Lieutenant McCann (five feet four inches and weighing 135 pounds) pulled the pins and then made the dash to safety, while he kept watch outside on the front step to ensure that the area was clear of captains, majors and colonels. Walter Ruff recalled:

Upon doing my duty and ensuring the coast was clear, I gave the signal to McCann to pull the pin. I heard the fuse pop and began counting and looking for him to turn the last corner. My vast military experience in grenades told me that in about five seconds, the whole lot ought to blow. After I reached the count of four, and still no Dabney, I decided that I had better go inside and see if he was in trouble. As I entered the hall at the first turn, I met him coming out, with, as the Englishman said, 'just dispatch'. There followed a tremendous explosion, coupled with a sheet of orange flame and much dust. When the debris had settled and we had composed ourselves, we went back inside to collect our spoils of war. The safe had toppled off of the table onto the floor. It was still firmly sealed shut, with just one tiny hole in its door. We had failed completely, but there was worse to come. The wall against which the safe had been standing was completely demolished and it seemed that our dumb-ass supply sergeant had stored the entire company kitchen and all the outgoing mail, in the room on the other side of the wall. The chaos was unbelievable. Lieutenant McCann and I dutifully reported to Headquarters that the building had received a direct hit from a German 88, and that things there seemed to be in a terrible mess.

Just down the river valley from the 'Ozarks' in Geilenkirchen were the 1st and 3rd Battalions of the 333rd Regiment. They spent 20 November clearing the enemy out of Suggerath and forming a firm base from which the 3rd Battalion would attack the next day.

The regiment's area was subjected to intermittent shelling throughout the day. Some companies fared worse than others. Dug in on the extreme left of the American positions, Company A seemed to be having rather a bad time. In one of the exposed trenches on the hill was John J. O'Malley:

Those of us who were true believers, had a chance to say many prayers during those dismal days. On the second day, when a German shell landed next to our foxhole and covered Junior and me with dirt and smoke, I thought that the end was nigh; but I was wrong. After the barrage had lifted, I stood up and looked around. I was amazed that no one had been killed or injured. One smiling face that I did see was that of Precilliano Cervantes, a rugged Hispanic-American from California. Before going overseas, Cervantes and I had discussed a book which had been written by a US Army chaplain entitled *There Are No Atheists In Foxholes*. The book was based on his experiences as an Army chaplain in Guadalcanal in 1942. Cervantes had told me at that time that he believed in neither a God nor an after-life and he thought that the book was bunk. As Cervantes and I stood in our foxholes like two prairie dogs looking at each other, I shouted to him, 'Cervantes, are you still an atheist?' He flashed a big grin and answered with one word: 'Yup!' That said it all.

Situation at 2400 hours, Monday, 20 November
There had been little new ground won during the day. The biggest achievement on the whole of XXX Corps' front was the 5th Dorsets' action in capturing 'Dorset Wood'. The rest of the 43rd Division had got nowhere. The rain, the mud and the enemy had seen to that. Neither had the Americans. The 334th Regiment still clung to the few hundred yards it had taken around Prummern, and the 333rd Regiment was consolidating the previous day's gains in preparation for the attack the next day. Operation Clipper, which had started so well, looked as though it was running out of steam.

Chapter Thirteen

The Attack Down the Wurm Valley

It was important that the 84th Division kept to the original phases of Operation Clipper and came into line with the US 2nd Armored Division in Gereonsweiler to protect its left flank. To do this, the villages of Mullendorf, Wurm and Beeck would have to be taken by the 'Railsplitters'. These three villages now became the day's objectives. Brigadier-General Bolling insisted that every unit in the line make an all-out effort to gain them.

The problem of Beeck was uppermost in General Bolling's thoughts. It had to be taken, of that there was no doubt. The question was how. For almost three days the 334th Regiment had been hammering away along the shortest route from Prummern to the village. It had not advanced very far. The 2nd Battalion was stuck on the hills between Prummern and Beeck; the 1st Battalion had been pulled out of the line; and the 3rd Battalion had stalled underneath the slopes of Mahogany Hill.

If the frontal route were proving too tough, then perhaps it was time to try to sidestep the village and come in from the rear. Bolling decided that the moment had arrived to commit the 'Ozarks' 405th Infantry Regiment to the action. He developed a plan which would take this regiment onto the ground to the north-east of Beeck. Initially, to provide a firm base from which to launch this attack, the high ground to the north of Apweiler would have to be taken. Bolling decided that the 405th's 3rd Battalion would advance out of Immendorf and seize this hill and that the 405th's 1st and 2nd Battalions would then drive home the attack on Beeck the next day.

In the meantime, his 334th Regiment would continue forcing its way along the old route. On 21 November, for the fourth day in succession, the 334th Regiment set out for Beeck. While the 1st Battalion was held as a Divisional reserve, the 2nd Battalion was ordered to continue its progress towards the village along the high ground to the northeast of Suggerath. The 3rd Battalion was to try once again to get there along the direct route, northwards from Prummern. This time, however, it was to by-pass the defenders on Mahogany Hill and leave them to be mopped up later. That decision was a mistake.

It was raining heavily as the 3rd Battalion slipped past the southern edge of the hill and attempted to advance across the open plateau towards its objective. Once again, it did not get far. The enemy-held hill above and to the rear looked down on the battalion's every movement. As expected, an artillery barrage was brought down on the battalion the moment it rounded the hill, forcing it to a shuddering halt. Ahead, two pillboxes on the northern side of Mahogany Hill joined in and brought more counter fire down on the doughboys.

Crocodile tanks from 141 RAC came forward to flame the pillboxes. Three tanks, two flame throwers and a Churchill gun tank, set out for the two bunkers. In one was a German 88mm anti-tank gun. In three successive shots, the gun wiped out the three British tanks lumbering towards it. Each of them burst into flames. For the 'Railsplitters' watching from the sidelines, there was no alternative but to dig in and pray.

The 2nd Battalion moved a few hundred yards closer to Beeck along the high ground overlooking the River Wurm. The advance lasted about half an hour. Each time the infantry crested a slight rise, there was always another enemy-held hill overlooking the battalion. In this area, from the vicinity of Beeck, the Germans used anti-aircraft and anti-tank guns against the American troops. The only escape from the accurate barrage was to go to ground again. Once more, the tired GIs scraped narrow foxholes in the muddy ground. No sooner were they completed than they started to fill with water.

The 2nd Battalion, the most exposed of all the troops in action with XXX Corps, was spending its fourth day in the open. The men had not seen shelter or hot food for over ninety-six hours. Seeping water poured into their trenches, over the tops of their weathershoes and up their legs. All day long they stood all in icy water sometimes up to the waist, constantly watching for the enemy. Understandably, the harsh weather conditions soon began taking a toll of the infantry. George Green of Company E was one of them:

It was very cold. We slept in cramped and uncomfortable surroundings, either in waterlogged holes or out in the open on top of the ground. When you stood up you felt like Frankenstein's monster, staggering about stiff-legged and in pain. The Germans had much better boots than the ones that we were issued with. We were forced to smear something called 'dubbin' on ours to help waterproof them. It did no good whatsoever; our feet were constantly wet. I began to have grave problems keeping up with the rest of the guys, not realising that my feet were slowly freezing. You could not go on sick call with trench-foot, so I finally went in to get a band aid for a blister on my heel. When I took off my boot at the battalion aid station, the medical officer immediately diagnosed my condition as 'severe bilateral trench-foot'. I was quickly evacuated and spent the next four months in hospital. My case was not bad enough to require amputation, but I had to learn to walk all over again.

Green's case was by no means unique. The efficiency of the whole battalion was in jeopardy because of the state of the going. The battalion that had begun the battle so well was now in real danger of collapse.

At 1200 hours, the 3rd Battalion of the 333rd Regiment began its attack down the Wurm Valley, its objectives being the villages of Mullendorf and Wurm. Company K was on the right, using the Geilenkirchen-Randerath road as its axis, while Company I was on the other side of the river, striking out along either side of the road and railway line that ran between Suggerath and Wurm.

The 3rd Battalion's Commander, Lieutenant-Colonel William Barrett, knew that the right hand side of the battalion's zone would be the most difficult. Just outside Suggerath was a gently sloping hill that ran north-eastwards alongside the road to Mullendorf and Wurm. The railway line was cut into this hill, about thirty feet above the road. Further up this slope were six pillboxes, each positioned to bring maximum fire down on the area between Suggerath and Mullendorf. Colonel Barrett ordered Company I to advance with one platoon on the valley floor, while two others moved along the hillside, clearing out the pillboxes as far as Mullendorf.

The ground which Company K was to advance over was flat open fields, bordered by hedges and trees. There were occasionally very small woods, but the trees were devoid of leaves and gave little cover. About four hundred yards from the start line was a large chateau with a number of outbuildings grouped around it. The enemy was thought to have fortified this castle, turning the building into a strongpoint.

The 333rd Regiment's 2nd Battalion was kept as the Divisional reserve, while the 1st Battalion continued to hold the valley, roughly along an east-west line through Suggerath. To assist Barrett's attacking battalion, two troops of tanks from the Sherwood Rangers Yeomanry were assigned to the two leading companies, although it was known that the ground in front of Suggerath would be very difficult for them. The direct route was along the two roads, but these were heavily mined. The ground was very wet and soft either side of the roads. It would be pointless to try to move across this terrain: the results would be predictable. Too many tanks had already bogged down in all the other quagmires around Geilenkirchen even to consider that there might be a chance of making it.

In addition to the gun tanks of the Sherwood Rangers, assault tanks and flame-throwing Crocodiles from 'Drew Force' were added to the battalion's firepower. If these could be got close to the pillboxes, the task might not be as difficult as first envisaged.

Company K had advanced about a hundred yards along the left hand route before it ran into trouble. 'My platoon was the lead platoon,' recalls Harold Leinbaugh. 'I thought it was a big honour to be chosen to go first. It wasn't until forty years later that I realised I had been talked into it.'

Lieutenant Leinbaugh's platoon had come under small arms fire from the hedgerows immediately in front of it. Small parties of German infantry, no more than about a dozen strong, were holding the edge of each field. As Company K set out across them, so the enemy would open up. These Germans were part of the resistance line. They were Volks Grenadiers, pushed onto the valley floor to delay the Americans. Up ahead and over in the pillboxes on the hillsides were the real defenders, the men of the 15th Panzer Grenadiers. The old men and young boys behind the hedges were expendable. The enemy knew that they could not stop the advance there in the fields.

Company K moved ahead cautiously. They were green troops, seeing action for the first time. The Company Commander, Captain George Gieszl, had been told by Battalion to keep his company level with Company I on the right. Colonel Barrett had explained that it was important that neither company should get too far ahead of the other. There was not much chance of that. By 1400 hours, both companies had hardly moved.

Further over to the right, Company I, led by Captain James Mitchell, was having trouble making progress towards Mullendorf. Its main problem was the line of six pillboxes overlooking the valley. The machine guns of Company M helped with fire from the edge of Suggerath, as did its mortars, but the ground that Mitchell's company was advancing over was treacherous. In the valley, the 1st Platoon was being harassed by machine gun fire from the pillboxes, while on the hill the 2nd Platoon crawled towards the first pillbox behind an artillery barrage. It was very slow going.

Company I needed tank support, but none had been able to find a suitable way up to where they were required. The railway line was the problem. The only safe way across the line was through the underpass in Suggerath. The difficulty was that it proved to be too narrow to allow Sherman tanks through. The AVRE Churchills could negotiate the tunnel, but hesitated to go forward to the ridge without the support of the heavier gun tanks. Their stumpy assault cannon would give no protection against enemy tanks or guns, nor could it be used as an offensive weapon, except at very short ranges. Colonel Barrett asked the British liaison officer, Lieutenant McClaren Stacy, to go and reconnoitre a route for the tanks.

Lieutenant-Colonel Barrett had watched the commencement of the attack from an observation post in a pillbox overlooking the start line. At 1400 hours, the Regimental Commander, Colonel Pedley, ordered Barrett back to the battalion command post in Suggerath, where he would be in less personal danger. Barrett was a little annoyed about this as he really wanted to be up with his leading troops. Nonetheless, he complied with the order and left his staff in the forward observation post (OP) to observe and direct.

In Barrett's Command Post (CP) in Suggerath was a Ninth Army historian called Captain John O'Grady. He kept a remarkable account of everything that happened in this headquarters during the 3rd Battalion's attack, including the telephone and radio messages to the forward companies.

At 1415 hours, Colonel Barrett contacted Company I and asked if it had committed its reserve platoon against the pillboxes. Captain Mitchell replied that he had not. 'You must keep advancing,' ordered Barrett. The Colonel was concerned with the criticism he was receiving from the Regimental Commander. The attack had been going for two hours and the companies had advanced only a hundred yards. He got through to his staff in the OP and told them to keep up the pressure on Company I. 'Keep talking to Mitchell, he's gotta move,' explained Barrett. 'They are sore back there [Regiment HQ] because we haven't taken Wurm yet.'

At 1420 hours, Mitchell called battalion and asked for the artillery to be lifted. Barrett agreed to it lifting two hundred yards, but told Mitchell to get his men advancing.

Mitchell's 2nd Platoon managed to close on the first pillbox, due largely to the tenacity of its officer, Lieutenant Kirksey. He personally led them right up to the fortification. Enemy mortar fire began to land all around them. The lieutenant was wounded in the arms and neck. Now leaderless, the platoon attempted to force the surrender of the Germans who had taken refuge in the box, but had little success. The men needed more fire support to help them. Mitchell radioed back that he was desperate for some tank support.

Once again, Barrett requested that the Sherwood Rangers do something to help. They were powerless. There was no way up to the pillboxes. However, two Shermans moved to the edge of Suggerath and fired a few rounds at the pillbox, scoring hits, but none penetrated. This firing drew the attention of some German 88mm guns further up the valley and soon high velocity shells started slamming into the buildings alongside the tanks. The Sherwood Rangers retreated back into the village.

When the British tank liaison officer, Lieutenant Stacy, returned to Barrett's CP, he had little good news for the colonel. He had not found any usable route up to the pillboxes. Barrett was desperate and again impressed upon the British officer the need to have tank support up with his men. Stacy left to confer with his tank commander.

Barrett now decided to commit his reserve company, Company L, to help out on the right flank. He called its young company commander up to his CP to give him the news. 'I'm going to have to commit you on the right,' the colonel explained. 'That's rough,' the young officer replied. 'Rough, shit!' exclaimed Barrett. 'It ain't rough, they just aren't advancing that's all.'

The company commander questioned the colonel. 'You want us to hit their rear guard from the right?' The colonel nodded in agreement. 'You then want us to fall back into Company I?' The colonel shook his head. 'If you fall back you'll run into a lot of artillery. You'll get plenty of artillery fire anyhow, don't let it pin you down.' 'Yes sir,' replied the lieutenant.

Barrett was still concerned that the officer did not understand how important his attack was. 'Don't go off half-cocked now,' he said. 'Come here to the map. Now go up under the railroad bridge to this ridge and push off. When will you be able to go?' asked Barrett. 'By 1500 hours,' was the answer.

The company commander left the CP. Barrett was not convinced that committing Company L would be the answer. 'Christ!' he exclaimed, 'I wish I could get some help. Doughboys can't fight those things out there.'

Barrett then got on to his forward OP and gave them a message to pass on to Company I. 'Tell Mitchell to go ahead with the other two platoons and leave one by the pillboxes to keep them buttoned up. For God's sake tell them to advance by fire and movement, infiltration, or anything. Get Company L up there on the ridge and push him off on the right flank, we gotta get that bunch going.'

Down on the valley floor, Company I's 1st Platoon was just inside the wooded area and was receiving counter fire from its front and left flank. The platoon was trying to advance across the face of the emplacements on the hill, right underneath their guns. There was little cover in the bare woods and the platoon was suffering because of it.

At around 1500 hours, Colonel Barrett received a visit from Major Lampkin from the 333rd Regiment's HQ. The Regimental Commander had sent him forward to see what was happening. The major asked Barrett if he would like some assistance with the telephone or radio. 'Hell no!' replied the colonel. 'I like to fight a war, only I'm in the wrong place [Suggerath] instead of up front.' Barrett was still angered that he was not allowed to be up where the action was.

After staying for about thirty minutes, Major Lampkin decided to return to the Regimental CP in Geilenkirchen. Lieutenant-Colonel Barrett gave him a message: 'Tell Colonel Pedley that these men are fighting and dying up here. No one is lying down, but we gotta have power to do this thing.'

By this time, Company K had made a little more progress. Another two hundred yards of open space had been crossed and the company was now coming under fire from the chateau up ahead of it. Machine guns inside the castle opened up on the infantry moving along the road and across the marshy fields. The resistance was slight and the whole company closed nervously on the large building. There was no artillery support, the men countered the enemy with the weapons they were carrying. Several of the Sherwood Rangers' tanks were on the main road, but they advanced cautiously, clearing mines as they went. The tanks raked the chateau with machine gun and 75mm shell fire.

Company K had been expecting the chateau at Leerodt to be heavily fortified. Everyone thought it would be a tough nut to crack. In the event, it was occupied without a struggle. The castle had been in German occupation, but most of the defenders had fled as the doughboys approached.

Captain Gieszl, Commander of Company K, was puzzled. The chateau was a natural defensive position and he was concerned as to why the enemy should choose to give it up so easily. It did not make immediate sense to him, but the answer was not long in coming.

Gieszl moved his company out of the chateau and into the fields to the north. It had advanced no more than fifty yards before the three platoons were raked with mortar and machine gun fire. Then the artillery shells came in, bursting right amongst the infantry. The Germans had been watching and waiting for the GIs to walk into a carefully arranged trap.

The enemy had the whole area targeted. He knew the range to the yard. The skilfully combined German fire cut right through Company K. All of the men dropped down onto the sodden earth and tried to scratch a hole in the dirt to escape the terrible fire. Leinbaugh remembers digging at the soil with his helmet in the front and his boots at the back, in an effort to get underground quickly. The position was hopeless. The company had stumbled into one of the Germans' main lines of defence. Gieszl had no choice but to bring his men back into the grounds of the chateau.

At around 1600 hours, Company K tried again, this time Gieszl was determined to catch the Germans unaware. His men were ordered out of their slit trenches and to race across the open ground, forming up as they moved. As predicted, the moment the enemy spotted the movement, German shells once again came screaming over, but the GIs were one step ahead of them this time and the barrage landed behind the attackers.

Company K passed through the fixed-fire zone and pressed out across the flat fields. It did not take the enemy long to readjust his sights and before very long the 'Railsplitters' were once again straddled with shellfire. Then machine gun fire from the pillboxes and hedgerows joined in. Company K staggered to a halt.

For a while the men were completely pinned down. Gieszl soon realised that his company was not going anywhere that day. Permission was granted by Battalion for the company to pull back to the chateau and dig in for the night.

Captain Mitchell's Company I also failed in its attack that afternoon. He got his 3rd Platoon up to the first two pillboxes, but the troops could not prise out the defenders. While clearing the trench system around the emplacements, the platoon commander, Lieutenant Hunt, was killed and the rest of the men withdrew under fire, leaving the body of their dead officer behind.

Late in the afternoon, some Churchill tanks did go through the underpass under the railway line and up onto the ridge next to the pillboxes. Although they got some shots off at the emplacements, they failed to neutralise them and were forced to pull back in the face of heavy 88mm fire from the hill in front of them.

Company I's predicament did not ease all afternoon. Artillery and mortar fire continued to fall on it. Down in the valley, the 1st Platoon had been unable to get far into the woods and had spent the entire time in shallow trenches under continual machine gun and sniper fire. Captain Mitchell decided to pull his entire company back to more favourable ground and dig in for the night. By 1700 hours, Company I was back on the start line just outside Suggerath.

The promised reinforcements had never arrived. Company L had been unable to relieve the pressure on Captain Mitchell's men. The company had taken far too long to form up and became disorganised shortly after it had moved out. Colonel Barrett was furious at this. He arranged for the company commander concerned to be relieved of his command.

Although the 1st Battalion was not involved in the attack, it was still in the line holding the area between Geilenkirchen and Suggerath. Company A continued to overlook the valley from its entrenched positions on the hill alongside the British.

From his foxhole, John J. O'Malley could see a lone jug of grog lying in the nearby grass. Since the company had been in the line for several days, some men had managed to accumulate a substantial ration of rum. This particular jug had withstood shot and shell without so much as a crack. It had probably been dropped by someone diving for cover who had not considered it worth risking life and limb to retrieve it. O'Malley felt differently about it:

> As I observed the jug, I considered the circumstances and reached two conclusions: first, since a person lives only once, he should live as well as he can, and second, everything that is worthwhile in life involves some price or risk. Guided by those principles, I climbed out of my foxhole and retrieved the rum, and believe me, it warmed the cockles of my heart!

On the British front that day there had been little action. However, preparations for the resumption of the attack were being made. Horrocks had told Thomas that his 43rd Division would have to keep abreast of the Americans advancing up the Wurm Valley. At the moment there was no problem, but the closer the 333rd Regiment got to Wurm, the more exposed its left flank would be. 214 Brigade would have to close up and occupy the villages of Hoven and Kraudorf.

Since meeting up with the Americans on the road out of Geilenkirchen on 19 November, the 5th Duke of Cornwall's Light Infantry had been holding the southern flank of the Wessex Division's positions. With the Americans in Suggerath, this flank was now safe. Brigadier Essame, Commander 214 Brigade, decided that the 5th DCLI would capture Hoven and Kraudorf. The battalion had been in action for four days and was not really at its best to go into the attack once again, but, to be fair to the brigadier, the 5th DCLI was all he had left. The 1st Worcestershires were holding Tripsrath, the 7th Somerset Light Infantry was in the woods next to Hocheid and the 5th Dorsets had been pulled out of the line and sent back into reserve.

Lieutenant-Colonel Taylor received advance warning from his brigadier that his battalion was to carry out the attack on Hoven and Kraudorf through Hocheid Wood. The wood was composed of two distinct parts, joined together by an open gap of scrubland. The southern part was under the control of the 7th Somerset Light Infantry, with the enemy holding a line a few hundred yards inside the northern half. Early that afternoon, Taylor went forward with his intelligence officer, David Willcocks, to have a good look at the ground his battalion would have to cover.

Protected by the remaining late autumn leaves on the trees, the two officers surveyed the scene across the gap, They were confronted by a depressing sight. All around lay the shattered debris of the previous actions by the Somersets. The Cornwalls would have to cross the open gap immediately after leaving their start line. There was no possibility of using surprise. But something of a more sinister nature bothered Colonel Taylor:

All my training and instinct warned me that this operation was unsound. The reasons were clear to me. My tired and understrength battalion, after a period of sustained action, was not in a fit state to launch another attack. The rifle companies, with the exception of C Company, were down to about sixty men, instead of about one hundred. The reinforcement system was not working smoothly.

Taylor felt that, though it was tactically sound for a battalion to attack on a narrow front backed by maximum fire power, it was essential that other battalions also attack to widen the frontage in a series of blows. He knew that this could be achieved by the time-switching of artillery support fire. But the plan to attack with a single battalion on the divisional front without the supporting actions of other battalions was unsound, as they would be forced to endure counter attacks, which was the German custom. He knew that the 5th DCLI would be likely to meet heavy defensive fire from the Siegfried Line sited on the high ground to the right. It was also doubtful, very doubtful, if tanks could give close fire support, and almost certainly no anti-tank guns could be sent up to the objective because of the mud.

Standing in the cover of a slit trench, Taylor dictated his objections to his intelligence officer. They were written down on a message pad and immediately dispatched to brigade headquarters.

Later in the day, Taylor arrived at the headquarters for the conference prior to the attack and saw Brigadier Essame. The Brigadier had been perturbed at the message he had received from the Cornwalls' commander. Essame had a high regard for Taylor and it was the first time that the colonel had ever shown opposition to any of his plans or orders. Taylor recalled:

> The Brigadier took me by the arm and walked me up and down the big tent. 'George,' he said kindly, 'I'm not asking your battalion to attack on its own, the Americans in the valley and on the high ground to your right will attack simultaneously in the direction of Wurm.' That being the case, I felt that I could no longer object.

The wood that the 5th Cornwalls would attack through, Hocheid Wood, was held by Lieutenant-Colonel Borradaile's 7th Somerset Light Infantry. The battalion had been in the woods for two days and they were not very pleased with the place. 'All the trees were blasted and broken,' recalls Sergeant Dan Robertson. 'Another night and still no food. Another dawn, no counter attack. Just the continual heavy mortar and shell fire. The last time we had suffered such "stonking" had been back in July in Normandy.' The conditions being endured by the 7th Somerset Light Infantry in the forest were appalling. On the third day, Robertson recollects that Colonel Borradaile came up to his positions and one of the lads mentioned to the CO that he was hungry.

It was not through lack of effort by those in the rear that hot food had failed to reach the men in the trenches. They had been trying since the first night to get carriers up with supplies, but all attempts had become bogged down along the single muddy track that led forward. The path was on the outside of the wood in full view of the enemy. Rain had turned this slippery thoroughfare into a treacherous avenue of destruction. Each vehicle attempting the journey ran a terrifying gauntlet of shell fire. It was hopeless. By the second day the track was impassable to any traffic. The only remaining way forward was on foot.

Colonel Borradaile arranged to send carrying parties up to the forward companies with 'hay boxes' of hot food. He suggested that, instead of the normal procedure of platoon commanders dishing out the food to the men, it would be served on a track at the rear of the positions that led from the edge of the wood. Robertson remembers that it would mean all the men having to leave their slits and would certainly involve more risk than their normal procedure, which would have meant only platoon commanders moving around the positions.

When the food arrived at the track, Robertson was given the job of dishing it out. Enemy infantry were dug in a short distance away and, as soon as they observed the Somersets' movements, they intensified their shelling of the area, suspecting either an attack or perhaps a withdrawal.

I was standing up on the track with all this fire raining down feeling quite naked. I was relieved when Company Sergeant Major Goode arrived and said he was the last and I could get the hell back to my hole. I dropped down into my platoon command post and sighed to myself, 'Thank God for that.' I had just lit up a cigarette when there was an almighty bang right overhead and I felt as though I had been kicked in the left thigh.

Robertson had survived unscathed out in the open while dishing out food but, once back in the comparative safety of his trench, he had been hit. He was bleeding profusely from a deep wound. One of his platoon tried to apply a tourniquet but, because the whole of his lower body was covered with blood, did so to the wrong leg. When Robertson remonstrated with the man, he thought he was delirious.

Five and a half hours were to pass before stretcher bearers were able to get to Robertson. It was a monumentally difficult task for them to stagger through the fifteen hundred yards of ankle deep mud from the aid station in Hocheid. They had tried to use the telephone lines up to the forward companies laid by the signallers as a guide, but these were being continually cut by the enemy shell fire.

When they lifted me out of my trench, the pain caused me to pass out. I came to later with rain beating down and branches smacking into my face. The stretcher bearers had lost direction in the thick woods and had no idea which way to go. I told them to carry straight on as we had a three-to-one chance of coming into friendly territory. We heard what sounded like tree felling and headed for that.

The Royal Engineers were cutting down trees and using their trunks to form a log road. The battalion had abandoned any thought of using the track on the outside of the wood and had decided to make its own route through the centre of the forest. The Somersets were further assisted by the arrival of four 'weasels' – high-sided metal vehicles with broad, lightly-built tracks running on rows of small rubber bogey wheels. They proved to be life-savers, able to cope with the treacherous mud and to get up to the forward positions. From then on, stretcher cases could be evacuated more easily.

In Tripsrath and on the rest of the Wessex Division's sector the shelling went on. There were no more counter attacks in the area. The enemy was doing all of his harassment from the safety of the Siegfried Line.

The cellars in Tripsrath helped to save many lives, for they were safe from all but the heaviest shells. There was, however, a limit to their use because the infantry could not fight from them. They were used as shelters by each section only when they were withdrawn from their slit trenches to feed or rest. With the enemy in such close contact, there was always the distinct possibility of counter attacks. Eric Tipping was in one of the trenches in Tripsrath:

> Being right up in the front line changes one's attitude in many ways, none more so than your approach to time itself. Time no longer was a factor in your life, it had been replaced by the need to survive this moment and this attack, knowing that if you did, you may not survive the next. Could you survive the one after that? And so on into the future. Being in a forward slit trench with nothing between you and the enemy and expecting them to counter attack at any moment can, even with the most powerful forces in support, concentrate the mind. Will the next moment be your last moment?

In the air above the River Wurm that day, 21 November, were British aircraft from No 83 Group, 2TAF. There to support the ground troops, the day's operations were summarised in the group's war diary by the sentence: 'All missions rendered abortive by weather.' The overcast skies prevented it giving the infantry of XXX Corps what could have been a knockout blow to the German opposition.

In order to support the 'Railsplitters' in Wurm and Beeck, a strong force of Typhoons, some armed with bombs and some with rockets, were briefed to attack the two villages at midday. A large number of squadrons was airborne and as many as five were over the area at one time, but the cloud conditions were such that the targets, though indicated by red smoke, could not be located. All the squadrons were forced to return to base.

One of the squadrons stayed in the area for over an hour and a half, vainly trying to get through the weather and only left when asked to do so by one of its own officers, who was controlling it from the Forward Control Post (FCP) at XXX Corps Headquarters.

Obviously, the pilots keenly felt that the reasons behind their inability to bomb these urgent targets located by the ground troops should be explained. An entry in their report states this lack of success should not be put down to lack of effort:

> To fly in what approximates to a London fog at 200 mph, with only occasional gaps through the cloud which makes the countryside hard to recognise, and meeting [as one squadron did] US aircraft without being sure in the thick cloud if they were friend or foe, lies behind the phrase 'sorties aborted'. It represents air support of the most gallant kind and should be recognised as such. Although results may appear to be nil, the presence of our aircraft in the air must badly affect the enemy's morale and take his eye off of the ball.

At 1100 hours that morning, the 3rd Battalion of the 405th Infantry Regiment set out from Immendorf for the high ground 1,500 yards north of Apweiler. The advance went exactly according to plan. Some enemy shelling interfered with its movements from time to time, but by mid–afternoon it was dug in on its objective. It was a fairly quiet introduction into battle for the battalion. It was not to be so for the other two Ozark battalions. For them, the next day would be sheer, bloody murder.

Situation at 1800 hours, Tuesday, 21 November
The day had been a nightmare. Five American battalions had been in action and four of them had gained only a few yards. None of the important trio of villages had been taken. Beeck, Mullendorf and Wurm had not yet seen an Allied soldier. The British had stayed put in their positions and suffered continuous shelling. The whole of XXX Corps' offensive had stalled. The enemy and the weather seemed to be conspiring against it.

On the extreme right, the 2nd Armored Division had taken Gereonsweiler and needed flank protection. It was vital that the village of Beeck be taken, and Lindern too if possible, to prevent the 2nd Armored and 102nd Division being hit by the enemy from the north. To strike this point home to all concerned, information was released that 10 SS Panzer Division had arrived in the area of Linnich. The calibre of the defending troops was improving by the hour. If the momentum of attack were not soon to improve, it might not have the chance to do so again for a long while.

Chapter Fourteen

Mullendorf and Beeck

Wednesday, 22 November 1944, was the day when everyone went all out for the villages of Beeck and Wurm. The US 84th and British 43rd Divisions together put six infantry battalions into the attack that day.

Down in the Wurm Valley, the 3rd Battalion of the 333rd Regiment resumed its move towards Mullendorf and Wurm. In addition, the 2nd Battalion, which up until then had been kept as the divisional reserve, assisted by advancing out of Prummern across the high plateau directly towards Wurm itself. The route took it behind the hill on which the six pillboxes holding up Company I were situated.

Captain George Felton had brought his 2nd Battalion company into Prummern the night before. 'It was getting dark', he recalled. 'Dead Germans, dead Americans and dead animals were all around. There was mud everywhere.' Felton bedded-down Company G in the ruined church, while he slept in the company headquarters in the preacher's house alongside. 'Same religious pamphlets as back home and yet Hitler was supposed to have destroyed all the churches!'

The attack pushed off at 1100 hours, with Company F, the 2nd Battalion, 333rd Regiment, on the left and Company G on the right next to the orchards outside Prummern. Company E was in reserve. Felton's company had a frontage of about three hundred yards. The 2nd and 3rd Platoons were in the lead, while Felton came behind with the 1st Platoon. Artillery fire started to fall all around the moment the troops had left the village.

It was pouring with rain as the Company Commander, dressed in an alligator raincoat, took his men out of the orchard and into the attack. The 2nd Platoon mistook its bearings and headed for the church steeple in Suggerath, instead of Wurm. Felton followed after the 3rd Platoon and expected the 1st Platoon to do the same. The incoming shells were deafening. After a while he looked round and found that there was no one behind him.

They had 'frozen' with fear back near the orchard and had gone to ground. I ran and crawled back though the sugar beets to find them. No one was around. I jumped into a foxhole on top of a dead German. I remember thinking that this was the way that I had seen it in the movies! I yelled out at what men I could see to 'keep moving'. Red tracer bullets from German machine guns were right overhead. We could see no sign of the enemy. The 2nd Platoon was not around.

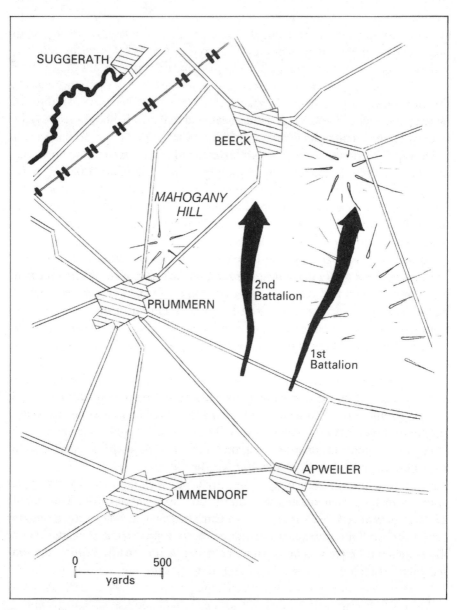

Map 7: 405th Regiment's Attack on Beeck.

Within minutes of the start line, Company G's attack was reduced to chaos. Felton's men had become scattered and disorganised by artillery, mortar and machine gun fire. The exposed fields gave no protection at all. The company commander requested new orders from Battalion. The reply was simple: 'Keep moving'.

Felton needed a safe place to regroup his men. About seventy-five yards ahead of him was a deep cut made by the road from Prummern to Beeck. He had his men make for that. In small groups they crawled across the open ground and into the safety of the road cutting. Frantically, the men dug foxholes in the wet earth, trying to get below ground before the Germans could retaliate. 'I knew that the artillery would soon come in,' recalls Captain Felton, 'and sure enough, within minutes mortars and shells began rocking the ground. One shell cut through the edge of the dirt at the top of the bank, skidded down to the road bed within ten feet of me and spun around fifteen or twenty times. Later I moved it so that no one would kick it and set it off. We were hard hit by the enemy.'

The fields that Company G was advancing over were coming under concentrated fire from the 102nd Panzer Artillery Regiment. Oberstleutnant Hoefer had his guns zeroed in on this open approach towards Beeck from the south west and, just as he had done with the other attacks on previous days, he pounded the ground with high explosive. His observers had a good view of the area from two pillboxes away to the right and could see every movement the Americans made. The 2nd Battalion was naked before Hoefer's guns.

The men of Company G spent the rest of the day and all that night crouching in their shallow trenches, away from the enemy fire. On its left, Company F fared a little better. Its intermediate objective on the way to the village of Wurm, was a group of pillboxes on the side of the plateau behind those that the 3rd Battalion was trying to capture.

Frank Freese was in the Weapons Platoon of Company F:

We took a pounding from small arms, artillery and mortar fire, starting the minute we left Prummern, which continued all the way across the open ground. At one time we were pinned down for over two hours unable to move. We had many casualties.

Freese was in the mortar squad in the rear and did not have to face the problem of convincing the Germans behind five feet of reinforced concrete that they were in more trouble than the doughboys out in the exposed fields. He remembers that there was no artillery or tank support to be seen, although it was on call if needed. The company attacked over open agricultural land with only minimal cover to be afforded by the slight gentle changes in topography.

The leading two rifle platoons reached the pillboxes and went straight into the attack. All of the pillboxes in this area had zig-zag communication trenches radiating out from them in different directions. Some led between adjacent pillboxes. The Germans seemed to do most of their defending from these trenches, the pillboxes themselves serving mainly as rest areas and safe havens for the wounded. Once the enemy had been driven from the trenches into the bunkers, they were seriously handicapped by a lack of all-round vision. There was a '*Kampfenraum*' at one end of each emplacement with a narrow opening for weapons. This provided a field of fire in one direction only. The pillboxes were supposed to be sited to give mutual support. There were, however, some flaws in this interactive defence system in this part of the Siegfried Line and the loss of one pillbox often left others uncovered.

In this case, Company F had come in on the blind side. Most of the fighting was done in the slit trenches. Those of the defenders who had retreated into the pillboxes were flushed out with fragmentation and smoke grenades. The bunkers were all captured, but at a price. When Freese got up to the emplacements later that day he was confronted with a harrowing sight:

> There were thirty-four bunks in the pillbox and every one of them was occupied by a wounded man. The same was true in the other pillboxes. During the night we helped carry the wounded back to an aid station in Suggerath. The deep mud and artillery fire made this an unpleasant and hazardous task. The mud also clogged up the actions of our weapons and even with constant cleaning the M1 rifles, carbines and machine guns were non-functional most of the time.

Company F had made the most successful attack on pillboxes since the swift gains on the first morning of the battle. It had done so with little artillery support and without the assistance of tanks. It was able to do so because its commander, Captain John F. Tye, kept his troops together and kept them on the move, a very difficult thing to do when under almost constant shell fire.

After the pillboxes had been captured, Tye took his men over the ridge to find Company I and join in its attack on Mullendorf. Captain Mitchell's company had been having another go at the pillboxes overlooking the river valley.

At 1030 hours that morning, a group of American engineers exercised their talent for demolition. A charge of TNT was placed in the middle of the underpass in Suggerath and fired. The explosion blew out the centre portion of the railway bridge. Subsequent charges removed the overhanging sides. The constriction on the road from Suggerath to the high ground had been removed, but the way was still blocked with rubble. The bulldozer, promised by Regiment to clear the mess, had not arrived.

The capture of the pillboxes along the hillside overlooking the river was the most important task facing Lieutenant-Colonel Barrett that morning. No one was going to be able to move from Suggerath to Wurm before they were eliminated. During the night an elaborate strategy had been evolved. The plan brought together artillery, armour and infantry in a carefully programmed attack.

First, at 1100 hours, the artillery would lay a barrage into the valley and the hillside, then gradually move it up onto the known locations of the enemy 88mm guns. The barrage would finally include smoke to shield the attack. Immediately behind the artillery fire would come the tanks – Crocodile flame-throwers and gun tanks to move both along the ridge and down the road, going straight for the pillboxes. Accompanying the armour would be Companies I and L. The infantry would sweep the hillside and the valley, capturing the fortifications. Then, it was all out for Mullendorf and on to Wurm.

Company K, on the far side of the valley, was to postpone its resumption of the attack from Chateau Leerodt, until Company I was abreast of it on the pillboxes. This would remove some of the enfilade which had caused so much trouble the previous day. On paper, the plan looked good. Barrett had real hopes that his battalion would achieve a breakthrough.

At 1110 hours, Colonel Barrett got through to Company I: 'Mitchell? Any of our artillery falling yet? No artillery yet! Well it should be soon.' The artillery fire was late starting. A short while after, another message came through to the CP. The colonel listened attentively, then turned to his aide and said aloud, 'Now here's the first mess up already, those tanks aren't out there yet.'

The bulldozer had not arrived in Suggerath to clear the blocked underpass. A row of tanks was waiting impatiently in the village for the order to move out. The 141st Regiment Royal Armoured Corps was putting two troops of Crocodiles and three Churchill gun tanks into the attack. In addition, there were two troops of Shermans from A Squadron of the Sherwood Rangers Yeomanry, plus five American M10 self-propelled anti-tank guns. All of this armour was stalled waiting for a single bulldozer.

Company I moved out without tank support. At 1200 hours, Captain Mitchell and his men jumped off once again against the same row of pillboxes. Following the losses of the previous day, two of his three rifle platoons were led by sergeants. 'Many of the men did not want to attack without the support they had been promised. They knew it would be the same as the day before,' recorded Captain Mitchell later.

The men of the company again came under machine gun and mortar fire the moment they showed themselves. The riflemen had to crawl every inch of the way. As the men had expected, it was just the same as the day before.

At 1250 hours, the underpass was finally cleared and the tanks set off to join Company I. A smoke screen laid on the far hill obscured the observation of most of the German 88mm guns and interference was light. The British flame-throwers soon joined with the 'Railsplitters' and things at last began to move, as Captain Mitchell explained:

The infantry-tank team began working on the first pillboxes. A few squirts from the flame-throwers and the Germans poured out of the two boxes and the trenches adjoining them. The bastards were afraid of the flame-throwers and would not be caught inside a box when one moves up. Initially, sixteen to eighteen prisoners came out of the first two boxes and later twenty came out of the third. We gave them all a chance to surrender, because we knew they would quit if given the opportunity. We didn't want to have to dig them out.

As the tanks flamed each pillbox in turn, Company I was able to move from one bunker to the next along the interconnecting trenches running between them. It was comparatively easy, even though the Crocodiles all lost their trailers which became bogged down in the mud and so had to rely on their guns to clear the last pillbox.

By late afternoon Mitchell had his men on the high ground overlooking the village of Mullendorf from the east. 'I tried to get the tanks to come with me into Mullendorf,' he commented, 'but the tank commander said they had no orders to go any further and they wouldn't go.'

Captain Tye had, by this time, brought some of his Company F up to join Mitchell and volunteered to follow him into Mullendorf. Both company commanders were keen to capture the village, but the odds were against them. The light was fading fast and the situation on the valley floor, and in the village itself, was uncertain. They were also receiving accurate small arms and artillery fire from Mullendorf.

Mitchell pulled his company back to a position in front of the pillboxes which he had just captured and they dug in for the night. The terrain there was more adapted to defence than the exposed hill above the village, even though it meant giving up a couple of hundred yards of recently captured ground.

Captain Tye did the same with Company F, although his defensive position was further back along the route he had advanced over. He also sent a patrol into Mullendorf to see what the defences were like. It never returned. Whether or not they made it to the village was not known. If they did, they were not the only 'Railsplitters' to get into Mullendorf that day, for Mitchell's 1st Platoon, under Sergeant Patches, had advanced along the river bank and entered the village.

Mitchell sent a small patrol after Sergeant Patches' men to see if it could get the platoon out, or at least locate it. The German defenders let off flares and had machine guns covering the outskirts. They caught the patrol in the open. The fire killed the patrol's leader, but the others managed to get back safely to report that there was no sign of the 1st Platoon and it had probably been captured.

There was a third company involved in the attack against the right hand side of the valley that day, Company L. Colonel Barrett wanted this company to go straight down the Suggerath-Mullendorf road into the village. This hazardous route would take it right under the faces of the six pillboxes on the hill above the railway line. However, by the time it was due to set out, Company I should have had the emplacements all captured. A new company commander, Lieutenant Richard W. Schupe, had been appointed to replace the one fired the day before. This would make the third commander Company L had had in four days.

Howard Hyle was a private in the 1st Platoon of Company L. He arrived at the company headquarters in Suggerath during the afternoon, bringing with him a new platoon leader who had just been posted to the company. He walked into the room just in time to hear the Battalion Commander conclude his orders to Lieutenant Schupe. Barrett was shouting at the young lieutenant, making it clear that he would not tolerate the same kind of 'foul up' as had happened the day before with the company. 'The pillboxes on the right have been taken; you will go straight down the road. The British tanks will lead you right into Mullendorf. I want you to keep going until you are pinned down.'

At around 1600 hours, Lieutenant Schupe led Company L through Suggerath to the rendezvous with the British tanks on the outskirts of Suggerath. Howard Hyle recalls that the lieutenant was actually running, with his men trailing behind him. It was cold and getting dark as the group of eighty infantrymen and four British tanks moved out past a pillbox on the right of the road which had been taken much earlier by the 1st Battalion. Hyle remembers seeing an American soldier from one of the other companies propped up at the entrance, wounded and crying. Bodies were lying in the drainage ditch.

Trouble started almost immediately the company began to move. The road to Mullendorf was known to have been mined and the leading Churchill gun tank from 141 RAC, crept slowly forward. Some of the anti-tank mines had been hastily laid and were clearly visible. The Churchill seemed to be heading directly for one of them. Horrified, the infantrymen shouted a warning. One of them, Private Roger Garst, ran over to the tank and grabbed the phone on the back of the Churchill to talk to the tankers inside, trying to get them to change course slightly to avoid the mine. While he was doing this, the tank hit the mine. The explosion blew off one of its tracks. Garst was injured in the blast.

The crippled Churchill blocked the road. Schupe tried to get the other tanks to go around it, but their commanders refused, claiming 'mud and mines' made it impossible. Exasperated, Schupe gathered his men and set off, running, across the fields towards the railway tracks.

The Company Commander was determined to get his men into Mullendorf. If the supporting arms could not help them, then they would do it on their own. Speed of attack would be his method. The troops ran all the way. Across the railway line, along the tracks beneath the six pillboxes, back across the railway, over the road, through the fields and into the buildings of Mullendorf itself.

There was some small arms and artillery fire aimed against them, but the lead platoon just kept on going. Others, further back, were not so lucky. The momentum there was beginning to flag and the follow-up platoons fell behind.

Howard Hyle was up with Schupe in the leading platoon.

> We were still platoons in a column – one squad right behind another as we ran on through an apple orchard into the little village. Our route took us along a path in sight of the river which was on our left. To our right were several houses. We made it into these, just as it was getting dark.

In the lead of one section was Dan McCullen and Ralph Williams. They burst into a small group of farm buildings on the edge of the village and surprised two Germans. The enemy soldiers were both wearing the black uniform of panzer troops. Mullendorf evidently had a first class German unit defending it.

Schupe now tried to contact Battalion and report his position. He was standing outside the first house on the edge of the village, by the side of the road that led to Kogenbroich. Alongside him was his radio operator, Private Rachofsky. Suddenly, there was a whistle, an explosion and the two men were lying dead on the ground. Howard Hyle saw it all:

> As we were inexperienced troops under fire, we immediately went for cover. Green as we were, we were not sure whether it was support artillery or enemy fire. In short order we got the right answer. Machine pistol fire and German tanks were heard coming down the street. Those of us remaining all headed in the same direction and found ourselves in an enclosed German farmyard, shut in on three sides, with the tanks closing on the fourth. There was no way out. We headed for the cellar and this became our prison.

The panzer grenadiers had no trouble flushing out the remnants of Company L who had made it to the village. Howard Hyle and the others went into captivity. Their fighting war had lasted just a few short hours. 'It is a shame that Schupe was killed,' recalls Hyle. 'He was born to be a hero; a real take-charge guy.'

On the other side of the Wurm Valley it was the same sort of day for Company K. Captain Gieszl and his men had spent the night under continual shell and mortar fire, in the grounds of Chateau Leerodt. In the morning, they picked themselves up and prepared to set off once more across the marshy fields, but there was a delay. The company was ordered to hold-up for a while until some progress had been made in capturing the pillboxes on the hillside overlooking the railway line. Finally, in the middle of the afternoon, word came from

Battalion for Company K to continue with its attack.

A supporting artillery barrage was laid in front of the company, twice as long, and twice as heavy, as the one that had preceded the attack the day before. When the shelling lifted, Company K set out from the chateau over those same open fields for the third time. Initially, the going was easy, several hundred yards were covered with only slight resistance. Then, while crossing one more open field, the riflemen were hit by small arms fire.

The enemy had another line of resistance behind yet another hedgerow. The fire ripped through the exposed doughboys. Lieutenant Bud Leinbaugh had his two sergeants shot dead beside him – both had bullets through the head. The infantry advanced on the Germans in a series of short rushes and broke through the hedge. Some of the Germans tried to make a run for it, but were mown down by the advancing Americans.

The company pushed its way forward through sheer weight of numbers, gradually taking one marshy field after another. Some tanks slowly inched along the road, their way cleared by engineers with mine sweeping equipment, but they were of little help. It was down to the riflemen themselves to carve their way through the German resistance.

Kogenbroich was reached. The small hamlet of a dozen houses was swiftly cleared of the enemy. Gieszl urged his men on. Their objective, Wurm, was just a few hundred yards away across the river. The men pressed forward, but the enemy was waiting – another line of Germans opened up with machine guns. Gieszl was hit and badly wounded, and the rest of the company was pinned down. It was by now almost dark. Any prospects of crossing the river and capturing Wurm that day had evaporated. Leinbaugh took over command of the company and pulled it back into Kogenbroich for the night.

Beeck is a name that will forever hold a unique place in the battle honours of the 405th Infantry Regiment. For the men who endured the fight for its possession, it is their own special calvary. There can be few regiments in the American Army who had such a terrible induction into the heat of war.

> At dawn on the 22nd November [recalls Irvin Citron], we pulled out of Immendorf and moved up to the front line in preparation for our first attack. We marched in single file through the fields, our eyes and ears wide open, our hearts beating wildly. It was raining hard.

The plan was simple – all plans usually are. The 1st and 2nd Battalions were to attack through the positions held by the 3rd Battalion 1,500 yards north of Apweiler. The 1st was to make for the high ground to the north east of Beeck, while the 2nd attacked the village from the south. Support would be given by tanks and artillery. The 3rd Battalion of the 334th Regiment would also continue with its own advance on the 405th's left flank. These three battalions were to make for Beeck at the same time.

'Hope you fellows have an easy day!' called out a GI from the 2nd Battalion as Fred Sutton and his fellow litter bearers walked past on their way up to the start line. Sutton called back that he hoped they would too. The general attitude was one of confidence. Some of the younger men were cracking jokes about how nice the picnic was going to be, although most were scared underneath and only wanted to bolster up their spirits. Sutton remembered his feelings:

> We were given no briefing except that we were making an attack. I had no idea about our objective, what opposition there was, or how grand a scale this attack was to be. These fellows had been in foxholes for over two weeks on defence and were now going into the biggest attack they were ever going to see, and the last that a lot of them were to see.

The 1st Battalion led the 'Ozarks' attack, with Company B and C abreast. Company A was in reserve. The two lead companies set off at 1030 hours, following behind a creeping artillery barrage. They swept down a steep-sided valley along the watercourse of a small stream and up onto a ridge on the right. This was where their troubles began. Artillery fire followed them up the slopes.

After a couple of hours in support, Company A was told to move on from its reserve position, along the small creek towards the other two companies. Irvin Citron was in one of the leading sections:

> As we moved out we saw several British tanks manoeuvring to get out of the mud. We marched along the creek which soon narrowed into a tree-lined gully. We could see a steep ridge in the distance; there were shells bursting on the top of it. The nearer we got to the ridge, the easier it was to make out that the men on the top under fire from the enemy artillery, were our buddies from the other companies. Suddenly, the battle broke on us too, as shells began to pour over the ridge and into the defile. Every man sought immediate protection; I jumped into the gully and almost landed on top of the body of a dead German soldier. We saw American dead there too. I did not look at them, I occupied myself trying to wash the mud off of my rifle until I could work the bolt back and forth.

From the gully, Citron watched the ridge and saw the men who were dug in on the side facing him, make sporadic rushes towards the top. There were Germans on the reverse slope. The artillery and machine gun fire was extremely heavy. Some men made it, others did not. Shells were landing all over the ridge and the gully in front of it. Citron and his section had little cover in the shallow watercourse and decided to make a break for a German pillbox about a third of the way up the ridge. During a slight lull in the shelling, they rushed up the slope and made it to an abandoned enemy bunker, just as another shower of shells poured down over the ridge.

Fred Sutton and the other litter bearers were also in action at this time:

> A fellow from Company A came back through and told me that he had seen a fellow get hit by the side of the tank that could be seen on the side of the hill to the left. So I took off running across the ground, crouching all the while. I found no one on the ground or in the deep tank track. After a search I found a helmet, rifle and a pool of blood. I yelled for him, but saw no one, so I took off back to the others. An officer shouted for me to keep down because I could be seen by the enemy. We had no medical markings other than a Red Cross brassard on my raincoat, which by then was covered with mud. I got scared then for the first time. I began to think of what could have happened.

Companies B and C moved over the ridge and down into the depression on the other side. Following behind, Company A took their place on the top of the ridge. Continual shell fire strafed the whole area. The 1st Battalion could not move and remained in these positions for the rest of the day, waiting for other units to come abreast of it and cover the flanks. Casualties began to mount. Fred Sutton and the other medics were kept very busy:

> One fellow was sitting on the bank of the stream with a bullet in his foot. He just sat there shaking with the pain and the cold. I found another in a tank track. I couldn't see him at first until I had got right up to him, because the tank track was a foot deep. A shell had hit him in the leg, tearing half of it off. I gave him morphine and bound him as best I could. There were several dead GIs in a group over to our left, who had been killed earlier in the morning. They were from 'Baker' Company and were left lying outside their foxholes in all kinds of positions. Some of them had been thrown out, after they had been killed, to make room for the other fellows.

On the left flank of the 1st Battalion, alongside the 334th Regiment, the 'Ozarks' 2nd Battalion had kicked off at the same time that morning. Companies E and G led the attack. Company F was in reserve. They advanced with tank support, but none of the armour was able to get beyond the first rise. German 88mm guns, dug in along the stone walls around the orchards on the southern edge of Beeck, raked the high ground with fire. Not one of the tanks was able to crest the shallow hill. The riflemen moved on alone.

Company E was stopped dead by the shelling and had its commander, Captain Knapic, killed. On the right flank, Company G worked its way along a slope and approached two pillboxes that were reported to have been neutralised. The report was false and bursts of machine gun fire raked the ground, forcing the company to dig in for protection.

During the afternoon, Company F joined in the advance with tank support. Moving forward with the Company Commander, Captain Peterson, was his radio operator Edward Souders:

> As the rifle squads moved forward, one tank pulled up behind us. By 1430, the tank had been knocked out by German 88mm fire from Beeck. Captain Peterson went forward alone about four hundred yards to the very front line and there, through the fog and the rain, he studied Beeck through his binoculars. Tremendous artillery fire continued to fall on the flanks of Companies E and G.

Using his map, the Captain took co-ordinates and directed Souders to transmit them 'in the clear' to Battalion. He also had the radio operator transmit them back to the 379th Field Artillery. Shortly afterwards, the whole ground shook as the American counter fire fell on the German positions. Company F moved forward behind it. As darkness fell, Peterson had his men within a hundred yards of the orchards on the south of Beeck.

Then the German mortars picked up their presence. The barrage was accurate and savage. 'We huddled together taking heavy casualties,' explained Edward Souders. 'I came across Private Wilcox, who had had his leg blown off by a direct hit. Nothing could be done to stop the dreadful flow of blood from the stump. He gave me his crucifix and asked that I take it to his parents in Grand Rapids, Minnesota, if I made it back. Captain Peterson and I stayed with him until he died from loss of blood.' The company commander pulled his men back towards the reverse side of the high ground. On the way, the captain was hit and wounded, as was Souders. By then, the company had dug in for the night. The men were covered in mud from head to feet, cold and hungry. Not one of them had a weapon in any condition to fire.

Some of the medics got the wounded back to the company area, where they were laid in the mud next to the foxholes. There was no morphine to help relieve their agonies. They lay in terrible pain on litters in the open. There was no way of getting them back to aid stations.

The 2nd Battalion had been ripped to pieces. Throughout the night there was no respite from the artillery fire. It was continual. The whole battalion cowered in waterlogged slit trenches and prayed.

Casualties during Operation Clipper had been high for both sides. For those British and American soldiers who had the misfortune to be injured, they did at least have the knowledge that their medical services were the best in the world. Once he had been extricated from the battlefield, a casualty had an excellent chance of survival. The casualty clearing stations and field hospitals just behind the front line saved hundreds of lives that otherwise would have been lost. Not so the Germans: by this time in the war the scarcity of supply was affecting all supporting arms. Although manned by men just as dedicated as those in the Allied forces, the German Army lacked the resources for an effective medical service at that late stage in the war.

As a result of serving with the Americans, Major Peter Selerie of the Sherwood Rangers had been evacuated through their channels when he had been injured on the second day of the battle. He remembers gaining consciousness in a US casualty clearing station. Adjusting his vision, he saw a bottle containing blood and a tube down to his good arm: At that moment the American surgeon bent down over him and said, 'How are you doing?' Selerie replied that he was doing alright … he wanted to know if that was a decent drop of blood that was being given to him. 'I'll have you know, Major,' the surgeon responded, 'that this is a rare old drop of rebel blood from way down South!' Ever since then, Peter Selerie admits to being a confirmed Confederate!

Harold Weaver was a Protestant chaplain with the 'Railsplitters' and remembers being summoned early one morning to the medical post in the nearby school house:

> I had been called because there was a young man in the centre who was expected to die. When I arrived I saw that there were many wounded soldiers sitting around the place, some in great pain. In the centre of the room was the young GI, lying on a table, with the doctor and several other medics; he had lost a lot of blood and was in a bad way. His blood vessels were flabby and flat and the medics could not get a needle into him to give him the life-sustaining plasma. I began to recite the 23rd Psalm to the unconscious soldier. When I came to the passage, 'though I walk through the valley of the shadow of death, I will feel no evil, for thou art with me…' the MD said to me 'He's repeating the words with you, ask him his name.' I did not know it at the time, but the young man's 'dog tag' had been lost and he might well have died as an unknown soldier. I found out the boy's name and, as I spoke to him, his blood vessels began to respond to the needle. He was able to take the transfusion and, although he lost an arm, he survived. I have always been impressed with the thought that this young fellow was brought from his unconscious state by hearing this statement of faith, which he must have learned as a boy, perhaps for confirmation.

Situation at 1800 hours, Wednesday, 22 November

Some gains had been made during the day, but the cost was far too high. The 333rd Regiment had advanced three hundred yards. It was abreast of Mullendorf, but did not have the village. Wurm was still an eternity away. The capture of Beeck was breaking the heart of the 405th Regiment; two of its battalions were dying in the mud on the hills to the south. The 334th Regiment now had only the 3rd Battalion in the line, and this still had one toe in Prummern. Over the other side of the river in the British sector, 'old Colonel George' was about to suffer his one defeat in the twenty actions that he fought during his long army career.

Chapter Fifteen

The Tragedy of Hoven

Lieutenant-Colonel George Taylor was a dedicated and professional soldier, a strict disciplinarian and a sound tactician. He was known affectionately as 'old Colonel George'. His battalion had had a very rough time since arriving in Normandy in June 1944. Always in the thick of the action, the 5th Duke of Cornwall's Light Infantry had lost two commanders killed before Taylor arrived from the 1st Worcestershires to take over the battalion.

In contrast to the new American troops fighting on the other side of the river, the 43rd Division's war had been long and difficult. Many of its men had been in uniform for over five years. Their first action, just like the one that the 'Rail-splitters' were even now enduring, had also developed into a battle of attrition. Losses throughout the summer continued to be high. Those men who had survived had become cautious. Discipline was good, and the troops fought doggedly when ordered, but experience had taught them when things were possible and when they were not. Colonel Taylor had grave misgivings about the 5th DCLI's attack on Hoven and Kraudorf.

Brigadier Essame originally planned to bring down a night bombardment on the area of woods in front of the 7th Somersets through which the Cornwalls would attack. However, Taylor feared that it would rob his troops of much needed sleep and probably give away any chance of surprise. So the artillery barrage was switched to the village of Straeten, to give the enemy the impression that an attack was going in there.

Artillery support for the action was to take the form of a block barrage starting two hundred and fifty yards from the edge of the wood past the gap. It was feared that by putting it any nearer to the attacking troops the shells might clip the tops of the trees as they descended and cause casualties among the leading platoons. To bridge the gap and secure the start line for the Cornwalls, the 7th Somerset Light Infantry was asked to shoot the battalion in at the edge of the woods with its Bren guns, 2-inch mortars and PIATS (the British equivalent of the bazooka anti-tank weapon) in case the enemy had moved forward some of their defence posts.

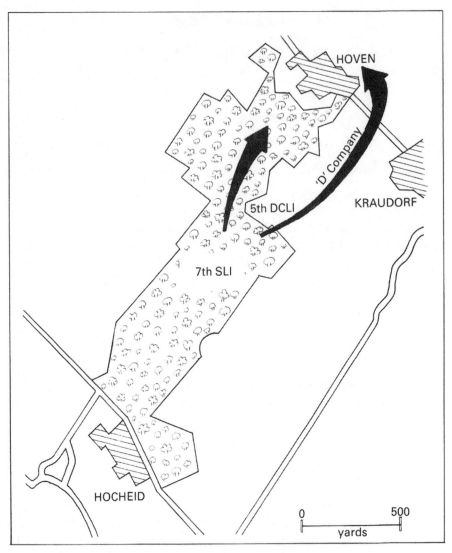

Map 8: The 5th Duke of Cornwall's Light Infantry's Attack on Hoven.

The plan was for C Company, the freshest company, to attack and secure the northern part of the wood. B Company was then to leap frog through and capture the village of Hoven. D Company, moving in the slipstream of this attack, would then cross the open ground under the cover of smoke and go into Kraudorf. This final operation was timed to take place after the wood had been cleared of the enemy, thus eliminating interference from the flank. Battalion reserve was to be a company of the Somersets. The 5th DCLI's own A

Company could not be relieved from its holding role overlooking the main road out of Geilenkirchen at Bruggerhof.

To support the Cornwalls, a squadron of tanks from the 4th/7th Royal Dragoon Guards would neutralise the edges of the wood and move forward to assist the attacks on the two villages. In addition, the open ground was to be swept by the heavy machine guns of the 8th Middlesex.

Colonel Taylor had decided that each company would be led in the attack by the seconds-in-command, so that the commanders could go back out of the line and get a good night's sleep. He knew that they would need to be fresh to meet the inevitable German counter attacks, which would probably constitute the crisis point of the battle. Taylor recalled:

> Our little command party moved forward to occupy the Command Post just behind the forward entrenched party of the Somersets. Owing to the tree roots, it was a miserable affair, only about three feet deep. We were in position an hour before H Hour, which was fixed for 1200 hours, to give the assault troops the maximum amount of rest. The artillery opened up on time and the men of C Company moved up to the edge of the wood. I was proud of them as they marched by. Dressed in their camouflaged smocks, they looked fresh and alert.

As soon as the leading troops had moved into the gap between the north and south sections of the wood, enemy machine guns opened up on them. The Germans had come forward as expected. Taylor could see everything from his advance command post:

> The firing rose to a crescendo of sound. The enemy were firing in long bursts. My brave men were falling fast. We could also hear the slower beat, beat of our Bren gun's answering fire. A few of our men made it into the northern wood and knocked out two enemy Spandaus, but they were killed in the attempt. B Company now joined in the firefight.

The artillery barrage had alerted the enemy to the impending attack and he began to respond with his own shell fire on the Cornwalls' forming-up place. In seconds, a salvo of shells fell among C Company, destroying the reserve platoon. Another shell knocked over Colonel Taylor and killed his signaller.

At this time, Major Kitchen had arrived from his rest camp and joined his company. As he explained later:

> The situation did not look healthy; 15 Platoon had ceased to exist. Moving with difficulty through bursting shells and small arms fire, I reached 14 Platoon, they had also suffered considerably. The shelling and mortar fire

was very heavy. In fact, neither before, including Hill 112, nor since, have I ever experienced such an intensity of fire.

Taylor had decided that C Company had shot its bolt as an attacking force. All that it could do was to hurl fire back at the enemy. The colonel knew that his attack had failed, so he devised a fresh plan. D Company was not now to attack Kraudorf, but to execute a right hook, moving outside the wood in the open under the cover of smoke, by-passing the Germans at the gap, before dodging back into the wood to head for Hoven.

D Company's second-in-command, Captain Spencer, executed Taylor's plan to perfection and took Hoven with a two-platoon pincer movement, getting into the village on the far side. Then the troubles began. Hoven was held by a company of the 15th Panzer Grenadiers. It fought stubbornly to retain possession of the village. Spencer's left hand platoon took the brunt of the resistance. It ran into a wall of rifle fire and a number of the Cornwalls were killed and injured. Throughout the afternoon, the struggle for Hoven went on. The village was never completely captured. Even as the light began to fade, some houses were still occupied by the enemy.

A radio message from Hoven told the Battalion Commander that D Company was on its objective. Taylor ordered the company from the 7th Somersets which had been attached to him up to reinforce the village. It never made it. The Somersets became bogged down in the fighting for the northern part of the woods. For a long while Taylor was not aware of this and did not realise that the company in Hoven was on its own. He also tried to get tanks up to the village, but none could even make it up to his Command Post.

In the late afternoon, Brigadier Essame, Commander 214 Brigade, came up to the Forward Command Post and saw Colonel Taylor. Essame obviously felt that Taylor had everything in hand and his battalion was on top of the situation. The battalion commander asked the brigadier for more men. He requested the return of his A Company. Essame agreed. The brigadier was later to write:

> Despite the large number of wounded struggling to extricate themselves from the tangle of woods, the high spirits of all ranks left a vivid impression. Taylor and his fellow officers might well have been at a rugger match at Twickenham rather than fighting a sanguinary battle, at close grips with the 15th Panzer Grenadier Division in a filthy German wood on a damp November afternoon.

Essame had every confidence in the ability of his battalion commander. He returned to his headquarters, secure in the knowledge that George Taylor's perseverance would pull the attack through. However, the reality was different. Taylor still had his doubts about the whole affair. He had the feeling that the brigadier's visit had clouded his judgement into thinking that the 5th DCLI could do anything. Without tanks and anti-tank guns to beat off the enemy, the battalion was dependent on hand-held PIATs and indirect fire from artillery to repulse any counter attack.

The battle in the woods, taking place only a few hundred yards from the Command Post, was rising in intensity. It was every bit as fierce as that going on in Hoven. A Company came up and joined in the action, but it was swallowed up in the dark forest.

During the evening, Taylor came to the conclusion that his battalion was holding on to a hopeless situation. He sent an officer back to Brigade Headquarters with a message for Essame: the 5th DCLI should be either reinforced or withdrawn. On his arrival there, the young lieutenant met the Corps Commander, General Horrocks, who had motored through the night in pouring rain to see the brigadier. Horrocks listened to the lieutenant give Taylor's report to Essame. The general was now aware of the great danger that threatened the Cornwalls in Hoven, stuck out a mile in front of the Americans on the right.

The two senior officers were under no illusions as to the critical nature of the situation. However, providing the Americans pushed on with their attack down the Wurm Valley early the next day, the German troops pressing the Cornwalls in Hoven would be outflanked. If the 5th DCLI were able to hold on, all would be well. If the Americans were not to advance, Taylor's men were doomed.

Horrocks left the final decision to the brigadier. If he wished to withdraw the DCLI while there was still time, he could do so. Essame thought for a moment and then declined. The battalion had lost too many men getting into Hoven; to pull them back now would be bad for morale. 'The DCLI,' wrote Essame later, 'had never since the early days in Normandy fought otherwise than to the bitter end. They would not do so now.' General Horrocks left the HQ and drove over to see Bolling at the 84th Division's Command Post. He urged the Brigadier-General to make one last urgent effort to take Mullendorf and Wurm.

During the night, Major Michael Lonsdale moved up through Hocheid Wood to rejoin his battalion.

After my rest in Brunssum, I went up to see Colonel Taylor at the Battalion Advance Command Post. At first he wanted to put me in command of one of the other companies that had lost its officer, but I insisted that I wanted to get back to my men in D Company. Taylor muttered something about me being 'a bloody Irishman', but let me go. He warned me that the company was about a mile into no-man's-land and he was not sure about the situation up there. I had arrived in time to make the journey up to Hoven together with a platoon of reinforcements from A Company led by Lieutenant Olding.

Major Lonsdale was met in the village by Sergeant Williams, who was acting platoon commander in one of the two platoons. The sergeant shook the major's hand and with a big grin on his rugged face said, 'Thank God you've arrived Sir.' The Company Commander asked what the position was in the village and was told that there was utmost confusion; the back of Hoven was being shared with the Germans. Casualties had been heavy.

Under the cover of darkness, Lonsdale met with Captain Spencer and re-organised the remaining men into two groups holding the houses on each side of the road facing, he hoped, the right direction. Then he went to see the casualties.

The wounded were all in the cellar of one of the houses. They were being cared for by a German doctor who spoke perfect English. He had spent some time during his training at St Thomas's Teaching Hospital in London. Lonsdale asked the doctor about the casualties and was told that some of the wounded were in a bad way. They would have to be evacuated as soon as possible. The major immediately organised this. Using some captured German stretchers and a few press-ganged prisoners, he formed carrying parties and sent the worst of the wounded back through the woods to safety. Lonsdale then turned to the German doctor and asked him about the German troop dispositions around the village. 'Major,' the doctor replied, 'I am fighting for my country, as you are fighting for yours. I am a doctor; you will get no information from me.' Lonsdale agreed with this statement and left the German to tend to his casualties. He did a fine job for them and undoubtedly saved many British lives.

When daylight came on Thursday, 23 November, the 'Railsplitters' went into action once more. Bolling had heeded the urging of the Corps Commander and the 333rd Regiment renewed its attack towards Wurm at 0700 hours. The 3rd Battalion was once more to make the main effort.

Lieutenant-Colonel Barrett was reluctant to let his infantry attack without tanks, but there was no choice. The roads were mined and the going over open country was too soft. Two tanks of the Sherwood Rangers had tried to go straight up the road from Suggerath to Mullendorf but had hit mines and were disabled. The engineers could not get up to clear the road of these mines because of the accurate enemy fire. The infantry would have to try once again on their own.

It was almost the same as the day before. Barrett sent Company L to take Mullendorf, and ordered Company K, assisted by Company C from the 1st Battalion, to cross the river from Kogenbroich to capture Wurm. The colonel spent all morning urging the British tank liaison officer to give some tank support to the infantry. The situation was hopeless and the tank commanders were reluctant to move. It was mid-afternoon before they relented and some tanks were eventually got up to exposed troops in Kogenbroich. By then,

Companies C and K were up to their necks in mud and the cold waters of the River Wurm.

The attack up the Wurm Valley was an exercise in frustration. More Americans were killed, but no new gains were made. The front line stayed roughly the same all day. The 'Railsplitters' had tried to take the pressure off the British 5th Duke of Cornwall's Light Infantry in Hoven, but they too had troubles of their own. The enemy resistance was just too great for riflemen to tackle on their own without tank support.

Just as it was getting light earlier that morning, over to the left in the small hamlet of Hoven, enemy soldiers began forming up for an attack on the besieged Cornwalls. They assembled along a hedgerow just outside the north-western end of the village. Major Lonsdale and his men could see them crouching behind the bushes about fifty yards away. The company's one surviving Bren gun was located in the last house in Hoven overlooking the hedge. The major told its operator to open up and move his fire down the hedge as though he were using a garden hosepipe, spraying the line of Germans as he went.

The light machine gun fire tore through the hedgerow cutting down the gathering enemy like a scythe. Then, for good measure, the gunner 'hosed' his way up the line again. The area behind the hedge went quiet.

A little later, the enemy tried once more. Major Lonsdale watched the approach:

> Instead of trying a different method, the Germans pushed another line of men up the same hedgerow and formed up in the same place. By that time we had managed to get a few magazines of ammunition together and so we gave them the same medicine again, firing down the row and then up again. The casualties were very heavy, bodies must have been piled up behind the hedge. This caused them to think a bit about the next attack. The Germans were not gaining any ground and I wasn't losing any. Obviously, they were getting bloody annoyed with me!

The next attack came from every direction. Infantry and tanks hit the village. Some of the enemy troops reached the company headquarters itself before they were beaten off. A grenade smashed the only radio set, cutting contact with the battalion headquarters and the guns in the rear.

A self-propelled gun manoeuvred out of the woods to the north-west and a tank came up the road from Kraudorf. There was so much mist, rain and 'muck' flying about that Major Lonsdale was not sure what was happening. All he knew was that he was being attacked by armour from two directions at once.

The tank on the road was engaged at close range by an infantryman with a PIAT. He got a direct hit and the tank stopped in the road, blocking the way into the village. One of the tankers was shot dead as he tried to get out of the turret. On the other side of Hoven the self-propelled gun was blasting out the walls of the houses, setting them alight. Then another tank entered the fray, coming across the open fields to approach the buildings.

Inside the company headquarters, pandemonium reigned. Wounded from both sides were everywhere. Shells crashed all around, deafening the signallers who were working frantically to repair the damaged wireless set so that the Battalion Command Post could be informed of the company's predicament and provide some artillery support.

Colonel Taylor could hear none of this action. No sound of the desperate fighting reached through the thickly wooded area between the village and the CP. The Battalion Commander was unaware that D Company was about to be eliminated.

Lonsdale's men were rapidly running out of ammunition. It was only a matter of time before they were overwhelmed. The dwindling number of survivors was using every bullet and grenade they could lay their hands on, including some taken from the wounded enemy soldiers. Every time the defensive fire began to slacken, so the German infantry and tanks came closer.

A second tank was heard coming down the main street. Captain Spencer later described what happened:

> I at once ran up the stairs with a PIAT. The tank was only twenty yards away. I leaned the PIAT against the window, took aim and fired. It was a mis-fire. The tank crew, seeing this movement, swung their gun in my direction. There was a great flash and I was temporarily blinded. Hit in the head, arm and legs, I crawled down the stairs and into the cellar.

Major Lonsdale now had little choice. It was either surrender or retreat. The company had fought almost to its last bullet. The major called his remaining men together. 'I told them that we had done well, but we were now, unfortunately, going to make a cut for it. We had to get out of Hoven.' He summed up their firepower: 'We had only a half a magazine of Bren ammunition between the lot of us.'

Through a hole in the wall blown by one of the German tanks, the major and all those who could walk made a break for it across the open ground and towards Hocheid Wood to rejoin the rest of the battalion. A tank saw the movement and opened fire, but it could not depress its gun sufficiently to hit the men right in front of it. The shell whistled over the Cornwalls' heads. Smoke from the blazing buildings blanketed the remainder of the escape route, until the safety of the trees was reached.

Major Lonsdale and nine men were all that came out of Hoven. They were the only survivors of the attack. Back in the village, the cellars were piled high with the dead and wounded of both sides.

We doubled as fast as we could until we saw a German twelve-man patrol moving right across our path. We stopped dead and dropped to the ground. Fortunately they did not see us. With only half a clip of Bren gun ammunition with us, I did not attempt to take them on! A little further on we ran into one of the Somersets. It was more dangerous getting into my own lines, than through the enemy's. This little chap was nervously manning his Bren gun on his own. I shouted to him, 'Stop, stop, stop,' and managed to get close enough to him to explain who I was. He could never have recognised us, we were covered in mud, in a filthy and haggard condition.

The survivors from Hoven passed by Dick Rutter of the 7th Somersets.

One man came back through our lines holding his arm. He seemed to be pleased with himself and happily told me that he had got a 'Blighty' – a wound that would ensure his being evacuated back to England. Poor chap, his arm was hanging by just a tendon and he was certain to lose it when, and if, he reached the regimental aid post.

Major Lonsdale found his way back to Lieutenant-Colonel Taylor and reported the situation. It was only then that the grim reality of the disaster sank in. The thought of this debacle remains with Taylor to this day: 'That was my one defeat. In the twenty actions that I fought during my career in the British Army, that was my one defeat.'

Taylor was still suffering from a sense of shock when he visited Brigadier Essame's headquarters later that day. General Horrocks must have realised this when he met the colonel. As he was leaving, Horrocks turned to Taylor and said, 'Don't blame yourself George, blame me.' Undoubtedly, he felt that he should have overruled Essame the previous night and got the 5th DCLI out of Hoven.

After the battle, Brigadier Essame saw Lonsdale and remarked: 'No wonder you got such a pasting in Hoven, the Germans needed that village. We later found out that they could overlook all of the Americans from there.'

Earlier that morning, the 2nd Battalion of the 333rd Regiment continued with its attack across the ground between the Wurm Valley and the line Prummern-Beeck. Its destination was Wurm, but the advance took it across the face of the German defenders in Beeck.

Company E marched out of Prummern and made a right turn across the fields towards the pillboxes. August E. Schmidt Jr remembers seeing the bunkers about a half a mile ahead.

As we reached a point a few hundred yards from the defences, we began to come under fire from the enemy guns around Beeck. With no cover to be had, and not knowing how to attack the pillboxes, our platoon leader told us to go back and take cover behind the banks that lined the road. I believe he was later relieved of his command for telling us to do this.

An hour or so later, a second attempt was made to capture the pillboxes. This time, the advance was covered by smoke from the 81mm mortars back in the rear. A small group went on ahead and managed to get on top of the bunkers. They knocked the top off of the air vents and dropped smoke grenades down the pipes, forcing the German defenders out.

During the battle, Major Hayden G. Jones, the assistant G-3 at the 84th Division's HQ was asked for his views on the surest method of attacking pillboxes. He favoured the use of tactical teams within rifle companies. He felt that in the past casualties had been high because too many men with no particular direction had grouped around the pillboxes being attacked. Many of these had been killed unnecessarily.

No pillbox has been made that could not be taken by twenty men, providing that each had a job to do and understood that job. If the twenty couldn't take the pillbox, then a hundred men would have no more success. They should, of course, have the benefit of the necessary assault weapons, notably tanks. Sometimes, there will be occasions when the infantry have no support. They will then be forced to keep the pillbox 'buttoned up' with rifle and automatic weapon fire, and work the engineers in with their explosives to blow the thing.

If this were so, it was a pity that each attacking company had not been given this information. Too many men had already been killed while trying to work out the best way of tackling these fortifications.

Situation at 1200 hours, Thursday, 23 November
The only battalion on the British side of the battlefield that had tried to advance since 20 November had been stopped and had been forced to withdraw right back to its start line with dreadful casualties. Everything on that side of the river favoured the German defenders. Major-General Thomas consolidated the positions of his 43rd (Wessex) Division and went into defence.

The 'Railsplitters' had much the same luck. Enemy resistance against them was dogged. The 333rd Regiment had made little progress either down the Wurm Valley or across the plateau west of Prummern. It was now up to the 'Ozarks' 405th Regiment to see if any progress could be made on this, the Americans' annual 'Thanksgiving Day'.

Chapter Sixteen

Retreat

Everyone on the battlefield seemed to be bogged down that morning and none more so than the two lead battalions of the 405th Regiment. The previous night, Company A 1st Battalion, was pulled back from the ridge to its original support position under the cover of darkness. 'We started out into the wet night,' recalls Irvin Citron, 'stumbling, slipping and falling into the mud as German machine gun fire whizzed over our heads. We finally made it the mile and a half back to the little bridge spanning the creek and beside a marooned British tank discussed our plans.'

There was nothing for the company to do but wait for more orders in the morning. The tired men hurriedly dug foxholes into the murky slime, with occasional bursts of enemy shellfire speeding their efforts along. Once the two-man holes had been dug, the GIs took turns to keep watch, while their partner snatched a few moments sleep in the waterlogged holes. Rain was still falling steadily to add to their misery.

At about four in the morning, Citron and the rest of his squad were roused from their sleep by the sergeant and told to carry some boxes of ammunition back up to the ridge they were on the day before. They were ordered to make sure they got the supplies there before daybreak. Each man had to leave his pack and food rations, but kept his rifle. The 30-calibre ammunition boxes were slung up on their shoulders and the squad set off across the stream towards the ridge. Citron remembers the journey well:

Across the creek, the struggling British tanks had left deep tracks in the oozing mud. Every time we took a step, we would sink in the ruts, the mud closing around us and our weapons as we tried to keep the ammo dry. We expended great effort in pulling one leg after the other out of the mud. At times I was in mud and water up to my waist, not able to move and had to be helped. It seemed like an eternity before we got out of the tank tracks and onto firmer ground. The boxes of ammunition weighed even more after all our exertions in the mud and our pace slowed down almost to a standstill. Daylight was breaking and we knew we would not get to our destination before dawn.

As the men caught their first glimpse of the ridge in the distance, so the Germans opened up with small arms fire. They all dropped into the mud but found no real refuge there. The daylight would make things even worse. There was nothing for it but to press on to the ridge.

It was light before they finally reached their destination. As soon as they arrived the inevitable enemy shell fire began to descend on the area. Citron made it to a nearby trench.

> There were three of us in a hole meant for one. The shells were landing very close and bullets were plunking away into the ground by the side of us. I looked up and saw the heads of two snipers against the skyline on the top of the ridge, which curved outward to our left. I started for my rifle, but I saw it was hopeless, my carbine was completely clogged with mud from the top of the barrel all the way down to the chamber. Everyone's rifle was in the same condition. We were in a hell of a fix.

The remainder of Company A now moved up to the front and despite intermittent artillery fire succeeded in spreading out all along the ridge. Citron was dismayed to find that the packs and rations belonging to his ammunition-carrying squad had been left behind, so they were all without food and water. 'I had nothing with me except my useless mud-clogged rifle and some rounds of ammunition,' he recalls. 'It was still raining when Lieutenant Barnik gave the order to move out.'

Company A was ordered over the top of the ridge to join the rest of the 1st Battalion in its attack. The moment the men showed themselves on the outline of the hill, things became much worse. Everyone was forced back into his hole as the shells came pouring in ever closer. 88's, 105's and mortars screamed into the ridge. Then German armour was heard moving up from Beeck. The German tanks began to engage the British tanks over to left rear. Citron saw three of these tanks catch fire. Small arms fire was coming in low over the heads of the men crouching in the trenches. Shells exploded so close that the concussion threw them about in their foxholes. Shrapnel was flying about everywhere. It was evident that the Germans were preparing a counter attack and the 'Ozarks' were caught on the hill without weapons that could fire.

In the valley on the other side of the ridge, Companies B and C had moved forward. Elements of Company B managed to advance across to the right and gain some high ground to the east of Beeck. It was a commanding position, overlooking the village, but it was very exposed. Runners were sent back to notify the battalion commander of the situation and the company settled down to await events. Opposition on this hill was slight. The enemy was making a counter attack south from Beeck and all of his artillery fire was heading that way.

More and more shell fire descended on the 405th and casualties continued to mount. A direct hit on a large trench in Company A's positions killed all six men inside. Away to the left, a German machine gun crew had worked their way forward and was strafing the area in enfilade. The regiment was taking a terrible pounding and more than one man gave way under the strain. 'Men were lying in their foxholes crying like babies,' recalls Irvin Citron. 'Both our company commander and the battalion commander were wounded.'

Earlier that morning, Wallace Katz of the 3rd Battalion's anti-tank platoon was driven up to a forward aid station located in a wooden shed. The shed was situated in a man-made excavation in the middle of a sugar beet field north of Apweiler. Katz and three others were given Red Cross arm bands and a stretcher. Placing a hand on Katz's shoulder, the battalion surgeon pointed to the north and told the four men to go and pick up the wounded from the 1st and 2nd Battalions who were located out there.

The small party crossed the beet field until they reached a steep bluff. Once there, they were spotted by men from the first two battalions who got out of their holes and began to call 'medic', indicating that they had wounded comrades. Some asked for morphine. Katz told them that his party were not medics but stretcher bearers and could only help remove casualties, not attend to their wounds.

They proceeded to carry one young soldier with a stomach wound down the hill, with Katz sliding on his rear end all the way down. They had soon accumulated about four wounded men at the bottom of the bluff and were met by a jeep that had driven along the path next to a drainage ditch. They placed the first of the wounded across the back of the jeep and were in the process of loading the young lad with the stomach wound across the hood when another stretcher team came up carrying a wounded battalion commander. The officer looked to be in a bad way and so they removed the young man from the jeep and placed the commander across the hood. The jeep then took off for the aid station, its driver promising to return for the others.

Meanwhile, further up the valley, the 1st Battalion was in dreadful trouble. The Germans were continuing to push forward with their own counter attack. The 10th Panzer Grenadier Regiment, supported by the 50th Heavy Tank Battalion, were bludgeoning their way forward. Passing low over their heads was concentrated anti-aircraft fire from the 287 Light Flak Battalion. Hauptmann Albert Schroder was using his light cannons in a ground support role to help shoot the panzer troops onto their target. Firing 40mm shells over open sights, the anti-aircraft guns on the high ground outside Beeck pounded the 'Ozarks' on the hill in front of them.

Away on the extreme right flank, the 1st Battalion's isolated Company B had been spotted and was left completely exposed on its forward-sloping hillside. It now came under direct fire from some enemy tanks and self-propelled guns. What cover they had became of little value as the enemy shells straddled the hill. The men were being slaughtered in the shallow holes which they had scraped in the ground.

Major Wilson R. Reed was the S-3 with the 379th Field Artillery Battalion back in Waurichen. The first indication of the enemy counter attack came through a plaintive report from one of the Forward Observation Officers with the 405th to the artillery. 'They are killing us in our foxholes,' cried the observer, and then, frantically: 'Send over some smoke, we gotta get out of here.'

Smoke on a battlefield has a double edge: it affords both sides cover. As such, usually it is controlled from a very high level. Major Reed now started four separate actions: first, ask Divisional Artillery for permission to fire smoke; second, ask the Regimental Commanding Officer if he wanted him to fire smoke; third, arrange for reinforcing artillery to give suppressive fire from its guns onto the attacking enemy; and, finally, prepare the battalion to fire the mission. Major Reed remembers what happened next:

> Very shortly, the answers came back. From Regimental CO, 'Give it to them if you can;' from reinforcing artillery, 'Firing in general area in front of infantry;' from battalion artillery, 'Laid and ready to fire!' and finally, from Divisional Artillery, 'Permission to fire smoke denied.'

For a moment, Reed did not know what to do. Then, with the pleas of the forward observer still ringing in his ears, he made his decision: 'Battalion, fire!' he ordered. In the course of the next few minutes, one hundred and twenty rounds of smoke shells landed on a four hundred yard line in front of the infantry. Another message from the forward observer: 'Keep it coming, oh God, keep it coming. We're heading out.' The company pulled back over the hill out of the way of the enemy armour. It took Reed over four months to 'expend' those one hundred and twenty rounds from the records, before he could finally draw replacement shells.

In Company A's positions, the situation was grim. At any moment, the men in the trenches expected to see the muzzles of the guns of German tanks poking over the hill before them and hordes of determined soldiers pouring down onto them. In fact, quite the opposite happened. Smoke shells began to explode to the front and the enemy fire started to wane. Something was up. The order had finally been given for the battalion to withdraw behind a protective smokescreen and head back to Immendorf. The Germans thought that an attack was being prepared and waited for the Americans to come at them through the fog. They did not realise the sad state that the 405th Regiment was in. The mounting casualties, the dreadful weather, the clogged weapons and news that the enemy had been reinforced all contributed to the decision to drop back. Irvin Citron in Company A watched his battalion start to pull out:

> The left flank of the battalion started moving out of their holes, one at a time. The word was passed along until it was our turn. Vyskocil and I climbed out of our hole and started back down the hill. I looked up to see a burst of German machine gun fire fell several men ahead of us on a slope as they climbed towards the top of the ridge. By this time the entire battalion was moving back at once. If the Germans could have seen this, there would have been a slaughter. But, aside from a few bursts of fire, they did very little to interfere. The day was waning as we kept plodding on. My feet were soaking wet and without any feeling, it was as though I had no legs at all from the waist down. Except for a few rotten green apples, I hadn't eaten for over twenty-four hours.

Wallace Katz and some other stretcher bearers waited in the gully below the ridge, but the jeep did not come back to pick up the wounded soldier they had been carrying. In the meantime, the young lad seemed to be getting much worse. Katz decided that they would have to carry him back to the rear. The six of them picked up the stretcher and started to head back along the drainage ditch. Despite the fact that the young man was small and light, and that there were more than enough of them to carry him, they made little headway. The sticky, glue-like consistency of the mud meant that every step they took required a great deal of effort. As one foot was freed, the other was sucked into the liquid clay. There was worse to come; the Germans sent a rolling barrage down the field.

> We carried the stretcher into the drainage ditch, placing the handles on either side of the ditch, just above the water level. We dunked the head of the kid with the stomach wound under the water for a moment while moving him and he complained that we shouldn't try to drown a wounded comrade. The barrage rolled up and down the field and we squatted as low in the ditch as we could, to escape the fire. A short time later, remnants from the 1st and 2nd Battalions retreated down the hill and motioned for us to join them.

Katz remained in the drainage ditch with the wounded, although the other stretcher bearers had left and joined in the withdrawal. He and another uninjured soldier looked after the wounded man in his care. Katz was still hoping that the jeep would return, when the Germans started shelling the field again.

> We took cover in the drainage ditch with the wounded and I watched the surface of the water being rained on by the clods of earth that were being thrown up by the exploding shells. My companion said that the bombardment was the preliminary to a German attack. He said he would remain with the wounded man and see that he received medical attention when the Germans came. I thought he was a very brave man, and I wasn't, so I decided that it was time for me to get out.

When Wallace Katz finally got back to the aid station, minus any casualties, he found the troops that had retreated before him lying around in ditches near the post. A surgeon came up to him and said that he knew he was tired, but there were fresh stretcher bearers and asked if Katz would lead them up to the front. 'What front?' replied Katz. 'Up to where the 1st and 2nd Battalions are,' said the doctor. Katz pointed to the men in the ditches. 'That's the 1st and 2nd Battalions.' The doctor was horrified. 'I never saw a heavy man move so fast,' recalled Katz. 'In less that sixty seconds, he was bugging out in his jeep.' Katz continued:

> Then the remnants of the 1st and 2nd Battalions started moving south again. When I realised that the aid station had been abandoned, I, too, decided to leave. On my way back, I passed officers standing by the roadside calling for men from the various companies and battalions to assemble in different places. I also spotted men from the 3rd Battalion preparing the small bridges across the ditches and streams for demolition. I continued walking back to my gun position and arrived there after dark.

Richard Roush was a stretcher bearer with the 3rd Battalion, 333rd Regiment. During the late afternoon, he had a call to go and pick some wounded from Company I's CP. The post was located in the last house in Suggerath on the left of the road to Wurm. As soon as Roush and his companion had reached the house, the enemy started shelling again. They took shelter in the basement just before the house was blown in on top of them. They survived, but the wounded men did not.

Roush came out of the ruined house and made his way along the road back to the aid station in Suggerath. While he was there a lieutenant came in and told all those inside that they were pulling out. 'Let's go,' he shouted, 'The Germans are coming after us with tanks.' Roush had never seen an aid station evacuated so quickly in all his life. The wounded were swiftly taken out and crammed onto a three-quarter ton Dodge. Everyone had a wounded man in his arms, one was even being held over the edge by his pistol belt. Roush jumped into the cab and took off down the road. He did not stop until he reached Geilenkirchen.

Late that afternoon, men started to come back into Suggerath stating that the Germans had broken through the American lines and were on their way. Gradually more and more men arrived in the village, including several walking wounded. They were all tired but very excited. Before long, troops from many different units were milling around. They had started to move further back down the road towards Geilenkirchen. Paul Howerter was a runner in the Company M Command Post and watched the scene unfold:

> Some seemed to be without their proper equipment which must have been abandoned or lost. The retreat quickly caught on and soon at least a hundred men were on what appeared to be a good mile run, trying to get back to Geilenkirchen. Some were able to hitch a ride on jeeps that were already loaded with four or five men. I was a nineteen year old and had been in the track team in school, so that when I, too, joined in, I was easily able to handle the run. However, I do remember pitying some of the older fellows, and those who were carrying equipment, who could not keep up with the race for safety.

Howerter and the others finally stopped when they reached the Regimental Headquarters in a barn on the outskirts of Geilenkirchen. There were men from several other companies congregating there. Finally, the officers got together to study the situation and were ordered by Colonel Pedley to go back and find out what the situation was.

Entry 651, timed at 1715 hours, in the S-1 Journal for the 333rd Regiment describes what had happened:

> 3rd Bn reported being forced back. A counter attack of tanks and infantry is reputed to have broken through L Cos. defences. Excitement terrific: 3rd Bn Hq and Hq Co retreated through Geilenkirchen but when situation was cleared up – found that one tank and 15 infantrymen made a counter attack and were forced back – our lines held.

It was left to Captain Burns to take a patrol from Company M back up to Suggerath and determine if the Germans had retaken the village. Private Paul Howerter was a member of that patrol.

The night was black, with no artificial moonlight to illuminate the area. Each man in the group had grave misgivings about driving back into Suggerath in the dark – they were sure there were Germans there. When the jeep drove into the village, it was parked under the arch of a courtyard. While Captain Burns and the others went off to check the command post Howerter was left to mind the vehicle with the help of a 50-calibre machine gun:

> In the black of night, I could not see my hand in front of my face. But I stayed there, mounting the machine gun which was on the jeep. I was shaking so much that I could not have pulled the trigger if I had wanted to. Many years later, at a reunion, I found out that this particular weapon was very unreliable and only fired intermittently. After about twenty minutes, which seemed like forever, Captain Burns came back and said things were OK and that there were no Germans.

Within an hour, the 3rd Battalion was back in Suggerath.

Situation at 1800 hours, Thursday, 23 November
Operation Clipper had stalled completely. The British had stopped and gone onto the defensive. Wurm, Mullendorf and Beeck were no nearer being captured than they had been three days ago. Enemy resistance had stiffened to the point that it seemed almost impossible to break. The reason was made clear when intelligence reports suggested that the 10th SS Panzer Division had gone into the line. The 22nd SS Panzer Grenadier Regiment had been seen in Beeck and Hoven.

Chapter Seventeen

The Rain, the Mud and the Blood

Although none of the men in the line knew it, at 1800 hours, Operation Clipper had come to a halt. Some changes had been made at the highest level. The combined Anglo-American assault on the Siegfried Line was over.

General Sir Miles Dempsey, Commander Second British Army, was Lieutenant-General Horrocks' boss. Two days previously, on 21 November, he had visited the Advance Headquarters of XXX Corps at Eigelshoven in Holland. Horrocks went over the current situation concerning Clipper and outlined some of the salient points with the Army Commander. Dempsey was not happy: 'The set up had become very mixed up,' he recorded in his notes.

On paper, he was right. The US 84th Division was under the operational control of the British XXX Corps. However, its 335th Regiment was attached to US 2nd Armored Division (having been moved from the 30th Division) as part of the US XIX Corps. In its place, the US 405th Infantry Regiment was attached to the 84th Division from the 102nd Division, which was part of XIII Corps. The whole thing was becoming an administrative nightmare. 'It is clearly time that the US XIII Corps took over the 84th and 102nd Divisions and got them separated from the 2nd Armored and properly sorted out,' remarked Dempsey. That afternoon, he motored over to the US Ninth Army Headquarters and spoke to General Bill Simpson.

Dempsey suggested that the 84th Division should be handed back to XIII Corps because the situation was getting very confusing and might easily become worse. Operation Clipper should be abandoned now that the Geilenkirchen salient had been removed. Simpson accepted his argument, but General Gillem, Commander of XIII Corps, said he could not do this until 1800 hours on 23 November. This was agreed.

So Operation Clipper finally stumbled to a close. The Anglo-American battle to break through the Westwall fortifications had come to a halt in the rain and the mud of a German winter. Its main objective, the elimination of the Geilenkirchen salient, had been achieved within two days of the start. The rest of the action had gained little and had cost so much.

Of course, this change in operational control did not mean that the fighting around Geilenkirchen immediately stopped – quite the opposite. The 84th Division continued with its struggle to capture the same objectives for the next four weeks. However, the British 43rd Division took no further part in the action. It remained in holding its positions on the left flank, until it was pulled out of the line in December.

Late in the day on 23rd November, Brigadier-General Bolling ordered the 84th Division to go over to the defensive. After a slight pause while the front line units were re-arranged, the 'Railsplitters' resumed the attack on 29 November with an assault on Lindern, the village behind and to the right of Beeck. Bolling had a new plan. If Mullendorf, Wurm and Beeck could not be taken from the front, then he would try to take them from the rear. Lindern fell that same day in a brilliant action by the 335th Regiment. Beeck was captured the next day. Wurm and Mullendorf lasted much longer. Enemy resistance in the two villages did not finally cease until 18 December, a full month after the start of Operation Clipper.

Horrocks had always regarded the battle for the Geilenkirchen salient as 'one of the hardest-fought actions of the whole war at the battalion, company and platoon level.' He was impressed by the extreme gallantry displayed by the 'raw GIs' of the US 84th Division, although he had some criticism of the administrative and staff arrangements. British officers involved in the battle were surprised by the apparent indifference shown by the American commanders to the physical needs of their men during this winter action.

Lack of provision of hot meals to the men in the line, and the prevention of trench-foot, seemed to be the main shortcomings of the American officers, according to the British. 'Hot food once a day, is as vital as ammunition,' claimed Brigadier Essame. The British were appalled by the number of cases of trench-foot, which is a preventable disease. The 'Railsplitters' had over five hundred non-battle casualties, most of which were from trench-foot.

This view was not necessarily shared by the Americans. Charles Hinds of the US 2nd Armored Division had observed the British way from close at hand during his experiences in North Africa, Sicily and Normandy:

The main difference, as I saw it, between taking care of the men in the British and American armies, was that in the British army, it was a paternal obligation on the part of the officers who were socially above the men; whereas in the American army, the paternal relationship was not that strong. Coming from America, the enlisted men were more self reliant and didn't necessarily think officers were their betters. College educations and/or high scores in intelligence tests, often determined most of the junior officers. But many enlisted men, like myself, felt closer to the men we lived and died with and chose to remain in the enlisted ranks. This was especially true towards the end of 1944 when new officers were in short supply. We could do without junior officers. In fact many small unit actions came to be run by enlisted men, who were generally more experienced and reliable than some of the replacements. That fall, especially, we had a lot of combat fatigue cases among the junior officers. So, from a British point of view, our officers didn't take care of the men properly. From our own point of view, we didn't ask anybody to take care of us.

Over sixty years after the event, this feeling still prevails amongst those who fought at Geilenkirchen. Mistakes were made in this, the first battle fought by the 84th and 102nd Divisions, but then again, most of the participants were new to action and they were still learning their trade. Those who survived were fortunate enough to profit from their mistakes.

Major Wilson R. Reed, 379th Field Artillery, 102nd Division, commented:

You will find no criticism of the higher officers voiced by me. While some of their actions and decisions may have cost lives and limbs, some delayed progress and others added to our misery, I am satisfied that all did their level best under the circumstances. We might have asked for more, but I do not think we should expect it. These were ordinary men who rose to extraordinary challenges, seeking to meet their obligations to their comrades. If that was not enough then so be it. I would be willing to go to war again with any one of them.

Most of the men who fought the Germans in the battle of Geilenkirchen were very young. They came from Christian countries with high ideals. They were taken from their homes and their families and were conscripted into a war that was against their inner beliefs.

Francis Mead, 405th Regiment, US 102nd Division, commented:

Early in the battle, a good friend of mine was killed. This incident had a profound effect on me. I learned the reality of war; kill or be killed. I had been raised Catholic and, like any good Christian, was taught from an early age, 'Thou shalt not kill'. Throughout my training I had often thought of this and how I would react when in combat. Seeing my friend lying dead on the road removed all doubt in my mind as to what I must, and would, do.

Many of these young soldiers gave their lives for their country and still lie in some foreign field. Others, who survived, still bear the scars both on their bodies and in their minds. James Meehan US 84th Division, commented:

So much of the war is clouded in the mists of time. The very bad I have pushed completely out of my mind; it is like something that I read about or heard about or something that did not happen to me. Such is the way we keep our sanity. I always felt that war made us all a little crazy and unless you could forget so much of it, it would eventually do you in.

For others, there were sights that will never be erased from their minds. Often, a poignant picture of an insignificant event remains captured in the memory, waiting to flood back unannounced in some still, quiet moment.

Benjamin Gerber, Anti–Tank Company, 405th Regiment, US 102 Division, commented:

I remember being very emotionally affected by walking through a minefield and observing the bodies of my buddies, some of whom were lying dead on their backs. The light snow that was falling on their faces gathered at their eyebrows and eyelashes and did not melt. That really bothered me for a long time.

Two American divisions had been blooded in battle with dreadful losses. The green troops had learned their lessons of war the hard way. Never again, throughout the rest of the campaign, were the 'Railsplitters' or the 'Ozarks' asked to pay such a high price. For the Wessexmen it was just another battle on their long, weary road to victory.

Frank Pinto, Company A, 334th Regiment, US 84th Division, summed up his memories:

I still remember the shock of seeing men killed in action and the cries of the wounded, calling for 'aid man'. The odour of the burning flesh of farm animals is still in my memory. The smell of over ripe unpicked cabbages and sugar beet in the muddy battlefield. The cold, the misery, the muddy foxholes, the trench feet and the fear; these are what I remember. But it was so long ago and so far away, it seems like a bad dream. I sometimes wonder if I was ever there.

XXX Corps Order of Battle

The differences between British and American formations can appear complicated. In both armies, the basic infantry division contained around fourteen thousand men organised on similar lines. Most confusion arises from the titles given to the various units.

The British infantry division is made up of three brigades of three rifle battalions each. In the American division, the equivalent of the brigade is the infantry regiment. This, also, comprises three infantry battalions each containing around nine hundred men. These battalions are further divided into four companies of almost two hundred men each, plus a headquarters company.

Each battalion of British infantry labels its rifle companies A, B, C and D. Each has its own platoon of small mortars and light machine guns. Heavy weapons are provided by a separate heavy weapon battalion which is attached to the division and distributed amongst the three brigades.

In an American infantry battalion, its companies are labelled according to the battalion number in the regiment. In the first battalion, the companies are A, B, C and D; in the second battalion companies are E, F, G and H; and in the third battalion companies are I, K, L and M. The first three companies in each battalion are rifle companies. The fourth company of each battalion, that is, D, H and M, are heavy weapons companies which contain 81mm and .3-inch calibre machine guns.

43rd Wessex Division

Brigades
129 Brigade
    4th Somerset Light Infantry
    4th Wiltshires
    5th Wiltshires

130 Brigade
    7th Hampshires
    4th Dorsets
    5th Dorsets

214 Brigade
    7th Somerset Light Infantry
    1st Worcestershires
    5th Duke of Cornwall's Light Infantry

Reconnaissance
43rd Reconnnaissance Regiment (5th
    Gloucestershire Regiment)

Artillery
94th Field Regiment RA
112th Field Regiment RA
179th Field Regiment RA
59th Anti-Tank Regiment RA
110th Light Anti-Aircraft Regiment RA

Engineers
43rd Division Royal Engineers
  260 Field Company RE
  204 Field Company RE
  553 Field Company RE
  207 Field Park Company RE

Signals
43rd Division Royal Signals

Machine Guns
8th Middlesex Machine Gun Battalion

Medical Services
Royal Army Medical Corps
  129 Field Ambulance RAMC
  130 Field Ambulance RAMC
  214 Field Ambulance RAMC
  14 Field Dressing Station RAMC
  15 Field Dressing Station RAMC
  38 Field Hygiene Unit RAMC
  306 Mobile Laundry and Bath Unit
    RAMC

Brigade Workshops
Royal Electrical and Mechanical
Engineers
  129 Brigade Workshop REME
  130 Brigade Workshop REME
  214 Brigade Workshop REME

Ordnance
Royal Army Ordnance Corps
  43 Division Ordnance Field Park
    RAOC

Support Services
Royal Army Service Corps
  504 Company RASC
  505 Company RASC
  506 Company RASC
  54 Company RASC

Divisional Provost Company
57th Provost Company
54th Field Cash Office
Postal and Education Officers

US 84th Infantry Division

Regiments
333rd Infantry Regiment
  1st Battalion   Companies A, B, C and D
  2nd Battalion   Companies E, F, G and H
  3rd Battalion   Companies I, K, L and M

334th Infantry Regiment
  1st Battalion   Companies A, B, C and D
  2nd Battalion   Companies E, F, G and H
  3rd Battalion   Companies I, K, L and M

405th Infantry Regiment*
  1st Battalion   Companies A, B, C and D
  2nd Battalion   Companies E, F, G and H
  3rd Battalion   Companies I, K, L and M

Divisional Artillery
325th Field Artillery Battalion   327th Field Artillery Battalion
326th Field Artillery Battalion   909th Field Artillery Battalion

Reconnaissance
84th Reconnaissance Troop

Engineers
309th Engineer Combat Battalion

Other Divisional Units
84th Signal Company
Headquarters and Headquarters
   Company

Divisional Support Command
784th Ordnance Light Maintenance
   Company
84th Quartermaster Company
309th Medical Battalion
Military Police Platoon
Band

Attachments to the 84th Division

Infantry
405th Regimental Combat Team from US 102nd Infantry Division

Armour
Sherwood Rangers Yeomanry (British) from British 8th Armoured Brigade**
'B' Squadron 1st Lothians and Border Yeomanry from British 79th Armoured Division
17th Tank Battalion from US 7th Armored Division
'A' Squadron (Crocodile flame-throwers) 141st Regiment Royal Armoured Corps from
   79th Armoured Division

Engineers
171st Engineer Combat Battalion
1st Platoon 989th Engineer Combat Battalion from US 102nd (Infantry) Division
A Squadron AVREs, 42nd Assault Regiment, Royal Engineers from British 79th
   Armoured Division

*Corps Artillery****
753rd Field Artillery Battalion
692nd Field Artillery Battalion
379th Field Artillery Battalion

Miscellaneous
357th Searchlight Battery Royal Artillery assigned to 43rd/84th Divisions at
Geilenkirchen

Notes
* The 84th Division's 335th Infantry Regiment was detached to 30th (Infantry)
Division, US XIX Corps, for Operation Queen, and therefore did not take part in
Clipper. It was 'replaced' for Clipper by the 405th Infantry Regiment from the US
102nd (Infantry) Division, US Ninth Army, which was under Bolling's control from
9am 17 November 1944, but could only be used in cases of emergency.

** Only A and B Squadrons Sherwood Rangers Yeomanry took part in the original
attack. Two other regiments of 8th Armoured Brigade – 417th Royal Dragoon Guards
and 13/18th Royal Hussars – were employed in the British side of Clipper battlefield.

*** XXX Corps Artillery.

Bibliography

Draper, Theodore, *The 84th Infantry Division in the Battle of Germany* (Viking Press, New York, NY, 1946).

Essame, Major-General Hubert, *The 43rd Wessex Division at War 1944–1945* (Clowes, London, 1952).

Hartwell, G.R., Pack, G.R. & Edwards, M.A., *The Story of the Fifth Battalion The Dorsetshire Regiment in North West Europe* (Henry Ling Printers, Dorchester, 1946).

Gill, R. & Groves, I. *Club Route in Europe* (Hannover, West Germany, 1946).

Godfrey, E.G., *The History of the Duke of Cornwall's Light Infantry 1939–1945* (Gale and Polden, London, 1946).

Horrocks, Lieutenant-General Sir Brian G., *Corps Commander* (Sidgwick and Jackson, 1977).

Leinbaugh, Harold P. & Campbell, John D., *The Men of Company K* (William Morrow, New York, 1985).

Lindsay, T.M., *Sherwood Rangers* (Burrup, Mathieson, London, 1952).

MacDonald, Charles B., *The Siegfried Line Campaign* (Washington, DC, 1963).

McMath, J S., *The Fifth Battalion The Wiltshire Regiment in NW Europe June 1944–May 1945* (Whitefriars Press, London, 1946).

Meredith, J.L., *The Story of the Seventh Battalion Somerset Light Infantry.*

Mick, Allan H., *With the 102nd Infantry Division Through Germany* (Washington, DC, 1946).

Montgomery, Field Marshal Sir Bernard L. *Normandy to the Baltic* (Hutchinson, London, 1947).

Parsons, A.D., Robbins, Colonel D.I.M. & Gilson, D.C. *The Maroon Square: A History of the 4th Battalion the Wiltshire Regiment* (Franey Co Ltd, London, 1948).

Watkins, G.J.B. *From Normandy to the Weser. The War History of the 4th Battalion Dorset Regiment* (Henry Ling Printers, Dorchester, 1946).

Watson, D.Y. *The First Battalion The Worcestershire Regiment in North West Europe.*

Wolff, Perry S., *Fortune Favored the Brave – A History of the 334th Infantry Regiment, 84th Division* (Germany, 1945).

Index